ROMANCE OF THE MISSION

ROMANCE OF THE MISSION

DECORATING IN THE MISSION STYLE

Elmo Baca

GIBBS·SMITH
P
PUBLISHER

SALT LAKE CITY

. . .

DEDICATED to the memory of my

mentors: Rheua Pearce, Ernie Olivas,

John Gavahan, and Antonio Sanchez

. . .

Text copyright © 1996 by Elmo Baca
Photograph copyrights as noted

00 99 98 5 4 3 2

Published by Gibbs Smith, Publisher
P.O. Box 667
Layton, Utah 84041

Designed by Traci O'Very Covey
Edited by Gail Yngve

Cover photograph by Dominique Vorillon

Printed in Korea

Library of Congress Cataloging-in-Publication Data

Baca, Elmo.
   Romance of the mission: decorating in the mission style / Elmo Baca. — 1st ed.

   p. cm.

   ISBN 0-87905-740-8

   1. Architecture, Domestic—Mission style. 2. Decoration and ornament—Mission style. 3. Mission furniture. I. Title.
NA7208.B3 1996
747'.9—dc20
                              95-45343
                                 CIP

CONTENTS

INTRODUCTION ·· 7

CLASSIC MISSION STYLE ·· 19

TEXAS AND
CALIFORNIA MISSIONS ·· 37

THE MISSION REVIVAL ·· 53

CLASSIC MISSION INTERIORS
OF THE CRAFTSMAN ERA ·· 73

MISSION STYLE —
TODAY AND TOMORROW ·· 97

ROMANCE OF THE
MISSION STYLE ·· 127

MISSION—STYLE RESOURCES ·· 142

No other American architectural or interior style can claim as long or as rich a tradition as the Mission style. The first expressions of Spanish Mission architecture in New Mexico

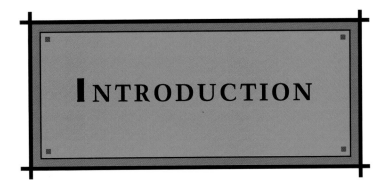

INTRODUCTION

were painstakingly crafted under impossible conditions by Pueblo Indians with the design, engineering, and supervision of Franciscan friars. Between 1600 and 1640, numerous massive churches of adobe and stone were erected in isolated Pueblo villages of the Rio Grande watershed. ••• While these mission churches were among the first European buildings built north of Mexico, they had long and deep roots in the cultures of Spain, Mexico, and North Africa. The true origins of the Mission style can be traced back to the eighth and ninth

The timeless look of a Mission-style veranda has been convincingly created by designer Michael Anderson in the Los Angeles home of Brian Gibson and Lynn Whitfield. Arches and walls were painted and sandblasted to achieve a time-weathered patina.

centuries, when Moorish armies of North Africa sailed across the narrow straights of Gibraltar and conquered the Iberian peninsula of Spain.

Islamic culture flourished in Spain, especially in the southernmost province of Andalusia. There in the great cities of Granada, Cordoba, and Sevilla, grand mosques and palaces were built in Mozarabic style, which blended the heavy stone and brick masonry of medieval Spanish buildings with the fine surface ornamentation characteristic of Islamic architecture.

North African artisans contributed many of the architectural and design techniques that have become hallmarks of the Mission style. Young boys in Morocco still apprentice in learning the intricate arts of inlaid mosaic tiles and painted glazed tiles that are essential to all Spanish styles of the Southwest, especially the Mission. Intricate wrought-iron work and elaborately carved ornamental plasterwork are other building arts inherited from the Moors. The Spaniards also carefully observed the Moorish art of building with sun-dried mud bricks, called adobe, which became essential in the dry climates of New Mexico, Arizona, Texas, and California.

Above all, the Moors demonstrated in Spain an impressive skill at building fortified palaces and compounds that defied Spanish knights for centuries. The awesome and regal Alhambra castle overlooking Granada included great courtyards, fountains, and gardens, which surely translated into Mission style in the Americas. Early mission complexes in Mexico and the Southwest were essentially self-sufficient fortresses whose architecture, planning, and massiveness were inspired by Moorish strongholds in Spain.

The creative techniques and inspiration for Mission architecture were developed in Spain for several centuries before Francisco Vásquez de Coronado's expedition first explored the American Southwest in 1540–42. The long Spanish struggle

An ancient and intricate Moorish doorway in Toledo, Spain, exemplifies the North African love of surface decoration that is a root influence of Mission style.

The 1902 Mission Inn of Riverside, California, built during the
heyday of the Mission Revival
period, incorporates Moorish,
Spanish, Spanish Colonial, and
Mexican design influences in its
exuberant and exotic facades.

to conquer the Moors evolved over the centuries into a fanatic holy war of
Christianity against Islam. For most Spaniards, the final conquest of Granada and
the banishment of the Moors from Europe in 1492 overshadowed the discovery of
new lands in the western sea by Christopher Columbus.

The triumph of Christianity in Spain thus set the stage for the Christian settlement of the Americas by "divine right." Gold was the object of greedy conquests,
and Indian slaves were justified by exaggerated reports to the king of "converted"
Indian souls. In this sad legacy, the missions played a vital role. As a technique of
domination, conquest, and territory control, the mission complexes enabled Spain
to rule vast areas of the world.

In the United States, these complexes were built not only as Christian outposts
but as military buffers as well. The Texas mission churches were a quick response
to encroaching French threats from Louisiana about 1750, and California's remarkable string of missions was built beginning in 1769 after rumors of Russian expansion plans from Alaska were reported to the Spanish viceroy in Mexico City.

MISSION SHRINES:
THE ALHAMBRA
GRANADA, SPAIN,
IN THE PROVINCE OF ANDALUSIA

...

The spiritual and aesthetic roots of Mission style reach back to the extraordinary period of Spanish history from 710 to 1492 during the Moorish cultural domination of the Iberian Peninsula. The complex fusion of architectural and decorative styles of Spain, incorporating Islamic, Roman, Christian, Hispanic, and Byzantine influences and producing an exotic and exuberant lifestyle, continues to inspire Mission designers.

Roman culture had long flourished in the southern Spanish province of Andalusia before Moorish invaders crossed the Straits of Gibraltar. In the ancient towns of Sevilla, Cordoba, and Granada, the basic Roman patio house with inner courtyard was adapted and embellished upon by the Moors. Simple, austere, exterior facades hid the rich pleasures of lush gardens, arcades, and baths within. This basic southern Spanish house form was transplanted into New World colonies, such as Chile, Mexico, and California, remaining the essential Spanish Colonial-style house.

The Moors perfected their building arts in Spain in great mosques and fortified royal palaces, many of which are still preserved today. The most famous example of the Moorish fortified palace is the Alhambra, or red citadel, that looms impressively over the city of Granada. Built after 1250 over a period of nearly two centuries, it provides numerous examples of building forms and techniques that have become standard aspects of Mission style. These include arcaded passageways, impressive arched door and window openings, towers, courtyards, formal gardens, fortified walls, and skylights.

Moorish designers and builders mastered the techniques of surface decoration, including mosaic tile work; plain, glazed tile work; fancy, painted tiles or *azulejos*; carved plaster and stucco work; and gilded, wooden parquet patterns. These art forms have been incorporated into romantic Mission style.

Astounding carved plaster reliefs and mosaic tile designs are combined to dazzling effect in the interior walls of the Alhambra.

A niche in the Alhambra is a brilliant example of carved plaster ornamentation.

In the architecture of the Alhambra, the tranquil courtyards and breezy arcades beloved by students of the Mission style find their inspiration.

In arid climates where the Mission style flourished, gardens were a treasured symbol of culture and refinement. The perfectly maintained gardens of the Alhambra recall the ideal of graceful living.

The Scottish Rite Temple of Santa Fe was built between 1909 and 1910 and is surely inspired by the Alhambra. The building's design closely resembles the forms of one of the Alhambra's great Gates of Justice.

Abstract and geometric designs of Moorish carved plasterwork on this doorway in Toledo, Spain, provide a design counterpoint to the baroque plasterwork of Mission churches created centuries later in the colonies of Spain.

A Mission Revival house in Santa
Monica, California, proudly displays its hallmarks: lush gardens,
tile roofs, and pristine stucco.

As a result, for two centuries, from about 1620 to 1820, Spain maintained a
tight control over her struggling colonies in the American Southwest and northern
Mexico mainly through the mission system. New Mexico's mission churches were
largely built in or near Pueblo Indian communities of the rugged high country near
Santa Fe and Albuquerque. Texas missions were concentrated in or near San
Antonio and El Paso. Arizona is home to only two lonely but magnificent mission
complexes near Tucson. California's twenty-one missions are located from San
Diego to San Francisco.

Largely because of the early strength and tenacity of the missions, communities of settlers, merchants, soldiers, and farmers settled nearby and, over a period
of time, developed into towns and, in some cases, world-class metropolises. The
Mission style itself has continued to find new expression over the centuries, transformed by major revivals and rediscovery, and today retains undisputed status as
one of the world's enduring architectural expressions.

Not limited to architecture, the Mission style has combined related arts, crafts,
and decorative arts to create a lifestyle that reflects and embodies the contemplative

In the entrance foyer of Brian Gibson's Los Angeles home, designer Michael Anderson rag-rubbed paint onto walls to achieve a worn-stone look. The painted *santo* on the central door is inspired by New Mexican religious folk art.

The arcaded cloister of the Santa Barbara Mission offers a Spanish Colonial-style scalloped bench for moments of rest and contemplation.

mood of the original missions. Beautiful gardens, simple and graceful architecture, solid furniture, honest materials of earth, wood, metal, and ceramic—all reinforce a look of timeless stability and peace of mind.

The Mission style is especially suited to the 1990s. After a decade of excess and glamour in the 1980s, many people, most notably "baby boomers," are seeking the basics of sturdy, quality housing; simple, refined design; and comfortable, durable home furnishings. Mission is a style that embodies these qualities while still fulfilling another intangible longing for tradition and romance.

The Mission style conjures up memories of the exotic and distant cultures of Morocco and North Africa, the ostentatious splendor of the Spanish empire, artistic genius of Southwestern Native Americans, Mexico's magnificent churches, and visions of paradise on earth, embodied by an unspoiled California. Just as the missions have overcome the ravages of time, conflicts, and the elements, Mission style endures in the hearts, minds, and homes of its devoted students.

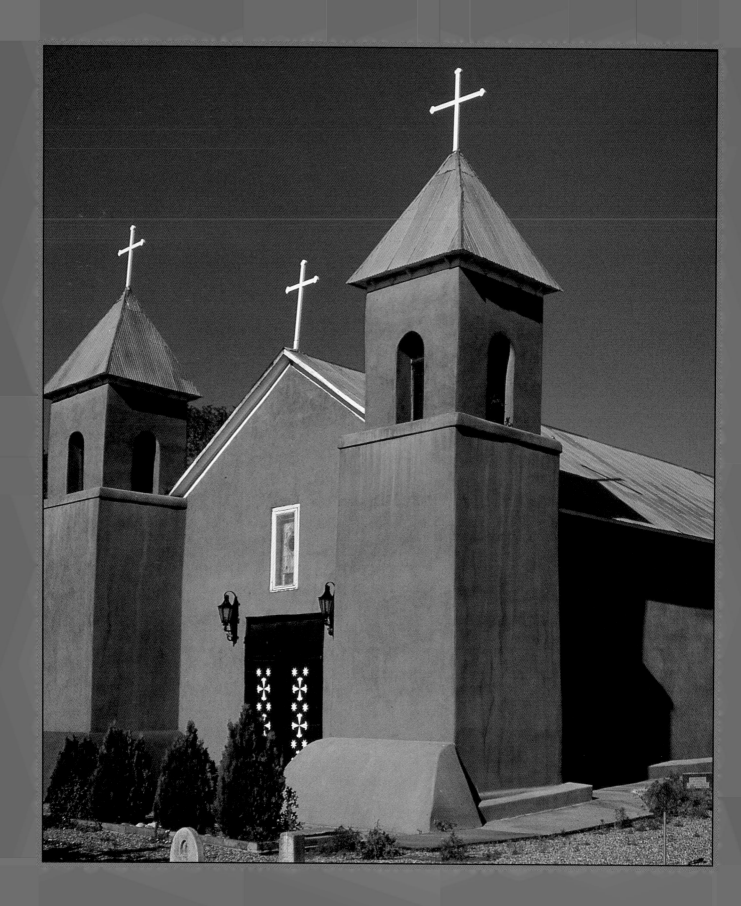

NEW MEXICO MISSIONS ··· After Coronado's failed expedition to the Southwest in search of the Seven Cities of Cibola from 1540–42, Spain's enthusiasm for a colony north of the Rio Grande faded for nearly fifty years. Fearing continued exploration and colonization of the New World by her European rivals and still wanting to believe in a fortune waiting to be discovered *mas allá* (farther on), the Mexican viceroy approved Don Juan de Onate's colonization expedition of New Mexico in 1598, nearly four hundred years ago. ··· Spain's first missionary efforts in New Mexico were tenuous and often violent. The Pueblo population had not yet been decimated by disease and warfare during the early seventeenth

CLASSIC MISSION STYLE

Spanish colonists began construction of the imposing Santa Cruz church near Española, New Mexico, in the early 1700s. Completed decades later, Santa Cruz still has many impressive works of Spanish colonial art within its grand interior.

The sculptural beauty of adobe attains the sublime in the organic forms of the church of San Francisco de Asis in Ranchos de Taos, New Mexico, which began construction about 1815.

century, and Spanish religious zeal was high. By 1616, Franciscan friars claimed 14,000 Indian converts and the construction of eleven churches. By 1630, Spanish reports (probably exaggerated) claimed that twenty-five missions had been expanded to ninety pueblos containing approximately 60,000 Pueblo Indians.

The largest and many of the most impressive missions of New Mexico were built during the early phases of the Spanish Colonial period between 1600 and 1680. A large and forced-labor community of Pueblo people was trained by the friars in the new technology of Mission architecture. Pueblo men were dispatched to nearby (and sometimes far-off) forests in the Sangre de Cristo Mountains to fell large timbers of ponderosa pine for the roof *vigas*, or beams, of the churches and other buildings. Only a meager supply of metal saws and axes was available for this brutal task.

Pueblo men, women, and children erected the walls of Mission-style churches, with the women applying and smoothing the final coats of mud plaster. For centuries before the arrival of the Spaniards, pueblo walls were built by the so-called "puddling technique," whereby balls of dried mud, with no binder such as straw or charcoal, were piled together in vertical rows to erect thin walls that were then

A magnificent adobe gate near Chimayó, New Mexico, complete with buttresses, wooden corbels, and a bell niche, mimics basic Mission forms.

The dramatic earthen buttresses of the apse of San Francisco de Asis church in Ranchos de Taos have been the subject of much artistic interpretation, including photographs by Ansel Adams and Paul Strand, and paintings by Georgia O'Keeffe.

21

"glued" together by an overall mud-plaster coat. These structures—the Pueblo villages themselves—were built directly on the ground with no foundation and little site preparation. Second, third, fourth, and even fifth stories were built upon each other in terracing style.

The traditional pueblo puddling technique of adobe construction has been described consistent with the coil-style pottery construction in which coils of clay are layered and shaped, plastered or glazed, and then fired. Pueblo walls were thin, and often upper-story rooms collapsed for lack of structural support. But for the Pueblo Indians, housing and architecture were perceived as secondary to nature; collapsed homes were simply abandoned or rebuilt.

The Spanish/European ideal of architecture contrasted sharply with the Pueblo world view and that of other Native Americans. For the Pueblos, life was meant to be lived outside, in direct contact with nature and the Great Spirit. Houses and other Native American shelters such as tepees, hogans, and lodges were not meant for dwelling but for protection from weather, animals, and enemies, and for storage of necessities such as food, clothing, and tools.

Pueblo architecture is organic and harmonious with nature. Pueblo villages and great communal apartment houses, including those at Zuñi, Taos, and Acoma, were organized and built in a sugar-cube massing style to resemble the forms of the surrounding natural landscape. Open ceremonial spaces in the center of the village or between major housing complexes became stages for magnificent religious ceremonies of costumed male and female dancers, honoring sacred animals or other natural phenomena. Sacred underground rooms called kivas provided private spaces for rituals, chanting, meditation, and meetings of religious societies and clans.

The Pueblo way of life had endured and flourished in this highly integrated way for perhaps one thousand years before the Europeans arrived.

Though the Spaniards preferred to build in stone and brick, they had become aware of the construction techniques and artistic possibilities of adobe architecture by observing the building arts of the Moors of North Africa. The friars chose to craft sun-dried mud bricks of rather large dimensions (about six to nine inches wide

The adobe houses of Acoma Pueblo, about fifty miles west of Albuquerque, New Mexico, displays the handcrafted walls and sugar-cube massing of Pueblo architecture that developed in the Southwest before the Europeans arrived.

A view of Zuñi Pueblo in 1903 by famed photographer Edward S. Curtis captures the remarkable communal architecture and lifestyle of Pueblo culture. A plaza (in the foreground) and terraced rooftops offer many opportunities for socializing, playing, food drying, and ceremonial dancing.

Sharing the fate of many Mission-style churches, Nuestra Señora de Guadalupe (Our Lady of Guadalupe) at Zuñi Pueblo, New Mexico, lay in ruins in this 1886 photograph. The church was rehabilitated in the 1960s by the National Park Service.

A splendid corbel from Zuñi Pueblo's Mission church of Nuestra Señora de Guadalupe displays Moorish-style chip-carving designs.

The interior of the church of San José de Gracia in Las Trampas, New Mexico, retains its essential Colonial integrity, as seen in this early twentieth-century photograph.

by twelve to eighteen inches long) instead of the dried mud balls used by the Pueblos.

Early Spanish missions in the Americas resembled fortress complexes with high walls, few windows, and heavy doors. In New Mexico, Spanish Colonial mission churches featured a narrow, single nave, sometimes with shallow transept chapels to resemble a cruciform. The altar end of the church, or the apse, was often rounded or battened. Roofs were flat and leaky, and sometimes featured a transverse clerestory window to deflect light onto the altar. In the earliest New Mexican mission churches, large *conventos* were attached to one side of the church nave. After the successful Pueblo Revolt of 1680 and subsequent reconquest of New Mexico by Diego de Vargas in 1692, the need for substantial *conventos* was reduced.

From the earliest years, Mission style in New Mexico has been characterized by primitive simplicity; naive, amateur folk art; and sculptural adobe walls. Walls were whitewashed with a gypsum slip coat called *yeso* or left plastered in natural earth colors. Yellow, red, and brown clay deposits used for the plaster coat could render the adobe with subtle color effects of yellow ocher, salmon, and coffee tones. Native American artists also painted decorations on the walls, featuring birds, animals, and stylized symbols.

Wooden architectural elements provided the friars and Pueblo artists with other creative opportunities. Pueblo men learned basic carpentry skills from the Spanish and were able to carve corbels, or *zapatas*, in pleasing scrolled shapes. Roof beams were often carved, or molded, or painted. The ceiling space between the beams was filled in with peeled and smoothed branches called *latillas*, which were laid in contrasting bands of color. The front doors of churches displayed many inventive expressions of carving, applied metal, wooden figures, inlaid panels, and painting.

Religious art of New Mexico contributes an important aspect of the classic Mission style. Few religious statues were transported to New Mexico from Spain and Mexico because of the forbidding overland Camino Real, the "Royal Road," of 1,800 miles from Mexico City to Santa Fe. Friars and a few saint-makers, or *santeros*, crafted crude but emotionally arresting figurines of the Catholic saints for use in the churches. Large altar pieces called *reredos* made in the seventeenth, eighteenth, and nineteenth centuries are still proudly displayed in the old churches.

After the initial colonization of Mexico and New Mexico was completed by about 1650, architectural styles for mission churches became more ornate, elaborate, and baroque. Many more skilled builders, artisans, and artists had arrived in Mexico, and baroque church architecture achieved dazzling effects of light, form, and color, often with gilded accents. High Mexican baroque style never reached New Mexico, but its graceful influence found its way to the northern Mexican province of Sonora, southern Arizona, Texas, and California in the second and third waves of Mission architecture in the Southwest.

The interiors of many Pueblo Mission churches in New Mexico have painted wall designs created by Native American artists.

SONORA MISSIONS—PADRE KINO'S LEGACY ••• The legacy of the Mission style in America includes many heroic figures, such as Padre Eusebio Francisco Kino, born Italian in 1645 and destined to become the leading Catholic

The parapet of Laguna Pueblo's Mission church of San José, gleaming beneath New Mexico's desert sun to passersby, has been described as a crown or Pueblo cloud design.

Pueblo painted designs create a unified decorative effect in the interior of the Mission church of San José at Laguna Pueblo, forty-five miles west of Albuquerque, New Mexico.

MISSION SHRINES:
SAN XAVIER DEL BAC
TUCSON, ARIZONA

...

The finest mission church in the United States is arguably the Mission of San Xavier del Bac, located a few miles southwest of Tucson, Arizona. Jesuit missionary Father Eusebio Francisco Kino first visited the Pima Indian village of Bac, or "where the waters gather," in 1692. There he found approximately 800 Sobaipuri Indians, tribe of the Pima, cultivating fields, much as their prehistoric ancestors, the Hohokam, had done centuries before.

Kino dreamed of a great mission church there, the crown of his chain of churches in northern Sonora, Mexico, and southern Arizona, known as the Pimeria Alta. Although Kino outlined the foundations for the great mission in 1700, he never saw the miraculous spectacle of the White Dove of the Desert.

Credit for building the mission is largely given to Father Juan Bautista Valderrain, a Franciscan priest who arrived at San Xavier in 1776, the same year the Spanish *presidio*, or army post, was moved from Tubac to Tucson. Consumed by the phenomenal building project, Valderrain died in 1790. Padre Juan Bautista Lorens supervised the 1797 completion of the complex.

San Xavier del Bac fascinates scholars of the Mission style because of its extraordinary complexity, baroque beauty, and lush decoration. It is apparent that trained architects and even entire guilds of quality Mexican craftsmen were employed in the design and finish work of the church, but basic structural work was completed by Pima Indians, supervised by the Franciscans. Stones for San Xavier were reportedly transported to the site over a distance of several miles from the nearby Santa Rita Mountains by women, who carried them on their heads.

Through the architecture of San Xavier del Bac, much of the entire legacy of North American Spanish-mission architecture can be traced back to its Iberian origins. In the ornate main portal, the exuberance and flourishes of the high Mexican baroque style are clearly evident. San Xavier boasts the finest Spanish Colonial dome in the Southwest, a form the Moors adopted from Byzantine examples and later introduced into Spain. The interior frescoes of San Xavier del Bac display rich colors and gilded effects that some scholars believe have Byzantine and even Persian sources. In its remarkable history and artistic splendor, the Mission of San Xavier del Bac is an eternal fountain of inspiration for practitioners of an eclectic Mission aesthetic.

The original polychrome design of the facade of San Xavier del Bac Mission is still evident in this photograph.

The splendor of Mexican baroque architecture is manifest in the Mission church of San Xavier del Bac near Tucson, completed in 1797.

missionary in northern Mexico. The Mexican province of Sonora, a traditionally large area located south of Phoenix and north of Hermosillo, Mexico, posed a daunting challenge to Spanish authorities, as it is an unbearably hot wasteland of limited natural resources.

Yet here in this rugged landscape of saguaro cactus and mesquite trees, Padre Kino established a string of at least a dozen mission churches and complexes, mostly in the present Mexican state of northern Sonora, and two in southern Arizona. Among his significant missionary accomplishments, Padre Kino was a tireless explorer and gifted geographer, who proved that Baja California was a peninsula and not an island.

Kino arrived in northern Sonora in March 1687 and began a nonstop crusade of twenty-four years of religious activity on behalf of the Jesuit order. Kino died in 1711 in the small village of Magdalena, Sonora, and is buried on the grounds of the Magdalena mission.

Padre Kino established the sites of the Sonora mission churches but did not oversee their construction. Many were built over several decades, with construction initiated under the supervision of Jesuit priests and completed by Franciscans after the Jesuits were banished from the Americas by royal order in 1767.

Padre Eusebio Francisco Kino established a chain of missions in the northern Mexican province of Sonora (south of Arizona) before his death in 1711.

The front entrance of the church of San Ignacio, fifty miles south of Nogales, displays a dynamic tension between charming folk designs and classical forms.

Built after his death, Kino's two mission churches that still survive in the United States are well known. San Xavier del Bac, located near Tucson, is the best preserved of the Sonora missions and is lovingly called the "white dove of the desert." The Tumacacori mission, located about twenty-five miles south of San Xavier, is a preserved ruin and national monument. The Sonora missions of northern Mexico located near the towns of Magdalena, Santa Ana, and Caborca are in various states of repair but offer students of the Mission style many fascinating architectural details.

The Sonoran missions are largely eighteenth-century provincial examples of Mexican baroque churches and share some kinship with the missions of Texas and California. In contrast to the austere mission churches of New Mexico, the Sonoran missions displayed a wealth of new building forms on the desert frontier.

From the exterior, the most obvious innovations are the soaring belfry towers and domes of Sonora, often articulated by graceful arched openings, buttresses, moldings, and lanterns. The Sonoran missions also have the conventional Mexican baroque fondness for the architectural decoration of the main entrance. The facade of Tucson's San Xavier del Bac church is ornamented with pilasters, carved-relief decorations, niches, and a broken, curvilinear parapet.

The Sonoran missions utilize various construction materials and methods in addition to basic adobe masonry. By the eighteenth century, brick kilns were more common, and many of the missions were faced with hard-fire brick and plastered with lime plaster on the interior and cement stucco on the exterior. Walls were usually whitewashed as a finish coat. Mesquite provided the major source of wood for planks and beams.

On the interior, the Sonoran missions present elaborate Spanish forms unknown in New Mexico. Ceiling vaults and domes sculpt the church interiors in graceful and rounded fashion. Interior walls are mostly plainly decorated but display niches and scalloped frames around doors, windows, and the altar. Altar walls are highly carved and painted.

In many ways, especially as demonstrated at San Xavier del Bac, the Sonoran missions express the zenith of the baroque Mission style in the Southwest. Some of the beautiful, curved, architectural shapes of the Sonoran desert, such as domes, vaults, and arcades, also appear on the Mission churches of Texas and California, but perhaps without the dramatic presentation of whitewashed silhouettes against the ruthless desert landscape and brilliant cobalt sky.

A wooden balcony over the main entrance of Tucson's San Xavier del Bac Mission is framed by ornate Mexican baroque plaster-relief designs, including the coat of arms of the Franciscan Order.

Heavily carved doors of the San Ignacio Mission bear Moorish carving designs such as rosettes and stylized pomegranate plants.

A bronze lion watches over the mission complex of San Xavier del Bac from atop a nearby look-out hill.

A Madonna found in San Xavier del Bac.

A Mission altar in San Xavier del Bac.

Ever since a tenacious band of shipwrecked Spaniards led by Alvar Nuñez Cabeza de Vaca and the North African manservant Esteban first wandered across Lone Star country

TEXAS AND CALIFORNIA MISSIONS

from 1528 to 1536, Texas remained a wild and unknown territory. By the mid-decades of the seventeenth century, Spain fully began to exploit the rich silver mines of northern Mexico, including Zacatecas and San Luis Potosi, and Texas gained importance as a military buffer on the northeast flank of New Spain. ••• Reports of French canoes on the Mississippi River in 1681 and 1682 caught the attention of Spain's rulers. Further French colonization activities near the mouth of the Mississippi in present-day Louisiana and failed French missions in East Texas near Matagorda

The magnificent mission of San José y San Miguel de Aguayo in San Antonio, Texas, was begun about 1720 and completed fifty years later. The facade was originally whitewashed and painted in a complex polychromatic design.

Bay compelled a Spanish colonial expedition to eastern Texas in 1690.

The first Spanish missions founded in Texas near present-day Houston and Nacogdoches never gained much permanence. Mexico City was a tortuous journey of three months away, and soon, continued French attacks began to take their toll on the morale and numbers of the Spaniards.

The beautiful hill country near the San Antonio River became more appealing for a permanent colony, and in May 1718, the Spanish established

The Alamo, Built 1718, San Antonio, Texas.

the Mission San Antonio de Valero and a nearby military outpost, the *presidio* (fort) and *villa* (village) of Bexar. Another mission, San Jose y San Miguel de Aguayo, was founded nearby in 1720.

The five San Antonio missions were built from 1720 to about 1780. As a group, the Texas missions were somewhat contemporary with Padre Kino's northern Sonora missions and preceded the great surge of California missions by a generation. The most famous San Antonio mission is, of course, the Alamo, otherwise known as San Antonio de Valero, but perhaps the most architecturally compelling mission is the intact San Jose y San Miguel de Aguayo, which has preserved its magnificent convento and cloisters.

The bountiful Texas country provided excellent building materials for the mission complexes. Good-quality limestone and great live oaks were utilized by Spanish builders to endow the mission churches with a sense of permanence and scale.

The San Antonio missions lay in ruins by the Civil War era. With the acquisition of the Alamo in 1883 by the state of Texas for $20,000, the great stone shrines of the San Antonio River began to gain supporters and patrons for their preservation. Today, the San Antonio missions reflect a spectrum of honey colors from their natural stone walls. Many of the conventional Spanish and Mexican baroque details are displayed, including the elaborate salomonic columns and shell niches of the Alamo and domed bell towers of Mission Nuestra Senora de la

The Mission of San Antonio de Valero, known as the Alamo, was founded in 1718, but construction of the familiar stone sanctuary was not begun until 1744. The mission was nearly ruined during the famous siege from February 23 to March 6, 1836, during the war for Texas independence.

now a Catholic Church 1810

▪ La Bahia

Purisima Concepcion, Our Lady of the Immaculate Conception.

Most interesting, however, is the fact that the San Antonio missions were gorgeously painted in brilliant schemes that incorporated natural pigments in the exterior plaster of the buildings—a frontier fresco technique that apparently used milk as a binder for the pigment before it was applied to the fresh plaster. Painted facade designs of the missions as rendered by engineer Ernst Schuchard in the 1930s display dazzling patterns of quatrefoils in a style that can be described as Mudejar, a blend of Moorish, Spanish, and Mexican styles.

While San Antonio lays claim to five great missions, the much-older Texas city of El Paso del Norte, the pass of the North, also maintains a rich legacy of colonial churches. The mission of Corpus Christi de Ysleta was founded in 1680, during the aftermath of New Mexico's Pueblo Revolt. Other El Paso missions—Nuestra Senora de Socorro, Our Lady of Divine Assistance, and San Elizario—were established in 1706 and 1727 respectively, but the present church buildings were built in the nineteenth century. The El Paso mission churches combine the austere, planar facades of New Mexico missions with strong baroque pediments and profiles on top.

CALIFORNIA MISSIONS ▪ ▪ ▪ The classic period of mission architecture in the United States rose and fell swiftly on California's fabled Pacific Coast; its lush beauty had been praised by Cabrillo in 1542, Sir Francis Drake in 1579, and Vizcaíno in 1602. Between 1600 and 1750, the great bays of Monterey and San Diego served the Spanish king as a refuge for the treasure-laden galleons from Manila; but otherwise, California was ignored.

Finally, Great Britain and Russia began to covet the great wealth of Spanish silver, spices, and tapestries that were shipped across the Pacific. Russian fur traders ventured down the Oregon coast as far south as San Francisco by 1765, and Captain Cook's Pacific adventures for England in the 1770s finally forced the Mexican viceroy to act. Don Gaspar de Portola, the governor of Baja California, and Padre Junípero Serra were dispatched to establish the first Spanish missions and settlements in Alta (Upper) California in the spring and summer of 1769.

Small and unassuming, with a broad and open face, Padre Junípero Serra seemed an unlikely choice for the hazards of the frontier, but he relished his task. When Padre Serra raised the cross over San Diego harbor on July 16, 1769, he was fifty-six years old. For the next fifteen years, until his death in 1784, Serra established a total of nine missions between San Francisco and San Diego and claimed a place in history as the founder of California.

Upon Padre Serra's death at the San Carlos mission in Monterey, the job of father-president of the California missions was given to Father Fermín Lasuén, an equally capable and dedicated Franciscan. Father Lasuén's eighteen-year reign produced an additional nine missions by 1798. The final two missions built in California under Spanish rule were Santa Inés in 1804 and San Rafael Arcangel (north of San Francisco) in 1817. The final Mexican mission of San Francisco Solano in Sonoma was built in 1823.

San Buenaventura Mission in Ventura, California, was completed in 1809. Nourished by a seven-mile-long aqueduct from the Ventura River survives one of the finest garden and orchard complexes in California before the gold rush.

The California missions represented the Spanish colonization, three-point strategy of mission/presidio/villa at its most effective. Unlike New Mexico, where missions were built in or next to existing Indian pueblos, California's Native Americans presented no existing villages or settlements. That the California missions were built from scratch and evolved into prosperous communities within just fifty years is a magnificent achievement.

It is difficult to speculate what the original California missions looked like, since many underwent considerable rehabilitations and romantic reconstructions after their tragic secularization and decline during the Mexican period of 1821 to 1846. Others were severely damaged by earthquakes and have been substantially rebuilt.

As a group of related buildings, the California missions offer a summation and climax of all previous Spanish mission architecture in the United States and northern Mexico. In some churches, echoes of the austerity of New Mexican missions appear. The exuberant baroque flourishes of Kino's Sonoran missions are also on grand display in some California sanctuaries as well as the imposing construction techniques of the Texas church complexes. What emerges from a careful look at the California missions is an architectural style full of historical and eclectic influences, both garishly polychromatic and severely minimal in decoration, assuming and reflecting the character of Moorish, Roman, Castilian, Gothic, and Mexican architecture in many splendid details.

The mission complexes of California introduced and made popular the forms and motifs of Spanish architecture that have become essential elements of contemporary architecture in the western United States. Among these are the love of ornamental entrances, as seen on the front facades of the churches, a convention that dates back to the Moors. The espa ada, or false front, of the church was built up with various styles of pediments such as curvilinear or triangular forms to make it appear more monumental. Another typical feature of the mission facade was the

Strong Moorish influence is seen in the courtyard and fountain of San Buenaventura Mission. The door design is said to be inspired by the Ventura landscape, with the upper line describing the hills behind the mission, and the lower curved lines representing the Ventura and Santa Clara Rivers.

An antique postcard depicts the nearly ruined condition of the Mission of San Carlos Borromeo in Carmel, California, in the 1880s, about the time California missions were rediscovered by preservationists and writers such as Helen Hunt Jackson.

campanario, or decorative wall openings to hang bells. Bell towers crowned by domes are also Mission-style hallmarks.

In plan, the mission compounds of California covered great sites, usually in a huge quadrangle, organized around a central courtyard that included the monastery, kitchen, stables, soldiers' quarters; workshops for blacksmithing, carpentry, weaving, and other industries; and granaries, vineyards, and dormitory rooms for some of the Indian converts. Often these great mission squares were framed by long and rhythmic corridors of arcaded columns, which formed attractive breezeways.

The enclosed patio with a garden or fountain is a beloved feature of the California Mission style, with direct association to Mexico, Spain, and ultimately to the desert gardens of North Africa. In the ruined glory of the fountain pool of the San Juan Capistrano mission, one can discern the ghost reflection of the Alhambra.

CALIFORNIA MISSION INTERIORS ••• In contrast to the popular misconception of the Mission style, which is one of simple white walls, clay roof tiles, and simple wooden furniture, the original California Mission style offers a remarkable palette of colors, textures, materials, and themes for artistic interpretation.

San Diego de Alcala, the first California mission, founded in 1769, is seen in this 1853 lithograph rendered by an army engineer. The lithograph captures the form of the mission's famous bell tower, which disappeared because of neglect after the Civil War and was restored in the 1930s.

Yankee merchant Thomas Larkin is credited with producing the first example of Monterey Territorial architecture, which combined Spanish/Mexican and New England building techniques. The house was built between 1836 and 1840 at the cost of five thousand dollars.

The great entrance doors of the Santa Barbara Mission are a beautifully proportioned exercise in classical design, order, and rhythm.

The wall openings of the cloister arcade of the Santa Barbara Mission provide a fascinating study in the pure geometry of cube, line, circle, and arc, characteristics of Mission architecture much admired by many designers.

Many people consider the noble facade of the Santa Barbara Mission to be the most beautiful of all California missions because of its classical style and refinement, symmetrical perfection, and subtle rose color.

MISSION OF SANTA BARBARA
SANTA BARBARA, CALIFORNIA
...

Before the twentieth century, the impressive Mission of Santa Barbara could be spotted for miles, perched upon its rocky hill called El Pedregoso by the Spanish. Modern developments have shrouded the famous church behind a veil of towering palm trees and charming Spanish Colonial Revival neighborhoods, but the luster of the mission's pastel rose-colored facade is undiminished.

Founded on December 4, 1786, by Father Fermín Lausén, successor of Padre Junípero Serra, the original church was destroyed by earthquake in 1812. The present structure was substantially completed by 1820. Today, the Santa Barbara Mission incorporates a Roman classical temple facade within the confines of two perfectly scaled bell towers, a design copied from a book on architecture by Vitruvius, produced during the first century in Rome. Later, Vitruvius's work was rediscovered in Italy during the Renaissance, influencing European design for several centuries. A copy of the Spanish edition of Vitruvius, published in Madrid in 1787, was found in the library of the Santa Barbara Mission.

Though substantial, what remains of the original Santa Barbara mission complex is only a fraction of the large Indian village, granary, tannery, and sophisticated water system that crowned the rocky hillside. A major earthquake in 1925 severely damaged the mission and destroyed much of Santa Barbara but proved to be a blessing. California rallied to raise $400,000 to reconstruct the mission, and Santa Barbara seized the opportunity to redesign itself in a Spanish Colonial image.

As two-thirds of the institutional and commercial buildings were destroyed, advocates of an integrated California architecture based on a southern Spanish, or Andalusian, prototype quickly prevailed upon the Santa Barbara city council to adopt an architectural ordinance enforced by the Architectural Board of Review. By 1930, the town of about 40,000 people had triumphantly emerged as a Spanish Mediterranean coastal oasis, a reputation it has perfected and upheld since. Santa Barbara remains a Mission-style mecca for true believers.

In frontier days, the long, impressive veranda of the Santa Barbara Mission offered a view of the Santa Barbara harbor and Pacific Ocean. Today it looks out upon a spectacular city park and neighborhoods of Mission Revival and Spanish Colonial Revival homes.

Church interiors of the California missions offer dazzling painted designs. Some are floral or inspired by other natural phenomena; some are architectural motifs such as columns, garlands, or painted ceiling beams; some are trompe l'oeil effects such as imitation marble or wood grain; and some, as in New Mexico, are inspired by Native American imagery and symbolism.

Mission Indians learned the arts of painting, fresco, stone masonry, stone and wood carving, and blacksmithing from Mexican craftsmen of New Spain. Organic pigments found in the soil, such as yellow ocher, burnt sienna, burnt umber, and vermilion provided a pleasing contrast for stronger colors of berries, moss, and other plants that the Indians favored.

During the early decades of the California missions, furniture and furnishings were sparse. A padre's room likely contained a bed made of planks, a trunk for clothing and books, perhaps a chair, and little else. Unlike New Mexico, California never developed a unique style of furniture or religious art during the Spanish Colonial era. By the early nineteenth century, the Camino Real of California, from Baja California to San Francisco, was well developed, and some household goods began to trickle into the missions and ranches of the Californios.

Wealthy families in the Spanish Colonial Southwest built private chapels in their homes. The restored chapel of the Olivas Adobe near Ventura retains much of its nineteenth-century character.

Whatever Hispanic furniture appeared in California would likely have been imported from Mexico. The heavily ornamented, carved, and scrolled styles of the Mexican baroque or Churrigueresque and rococo were favored in Mexico until about 1800, even as the rest of Europe and the new United States of America were turning enthusiastically to neoclassical styles such as Chippendale and French Empire.

Typical Hispanic furniture in the missions and ranches of California would have included a *sillon*, or priest's chair—an oversized armchair sometimes upholstered with leather or maybe even velvet. Simple side chairs might boast turned spindles set between back splats with some Mudejar, or Moorish, chip carving. Tables were simple and one of the few examples of carpentry that the mission Indians could produce. Church pews and benches were crafted in a modest decorative style, which perhaps displayed scalloped back rails and front skirts and curved armrests.

The most elaborate furnishings in Spanish Colonial California were storage chests, *armarios* (armoires), and beds. Mexican craftsmen have produced fine examples of painted and carved chests since the sixteenth century, and undoubtedly these useful containers were lugged or shipped to the earliest settlements. Heavy and highly ornamented *armarios* served the missions as storage for vestments but

A pie safe dominates the kitchen of the restored Olivas Adobe near Ventura. The punched metal and wood cabinet was imported by sea from the East Coast and became a favorite cabinet in well-to-do California households during the gold-rush era.

later found their way to prosperous ranches as the California-Boston trade in cowhides began to flourish after 1820. Some fancy painted beds with turned poster spindles appeared in California at the end of the mission era.

**TRANSITION TO A NEW CALIFORNIA STYLE ··· ** Even during the mission era, California attracted attention and influences from far-reaching places. The Manila galleons laden with exotic luxuries sailed by California's emerging ports on their way to Mexico. Rich tapestries and silks, the famous blue ceramics of China, rugs, and other oriental home furnishings found their way into the homes of prosperous colonists. Years later, during the era of the great clipper ships in the nineteenth century, oriental goods became commonplace in many California homes.

Other foreign products began to arrive in California by ship shortly after 1800. A booming cattle industry on the California ranches lured New England manufacturing companies searching for cheap hides for leather goods, especially shoes. A business partnership between the Californios and American entrepreneurs during the waning years of the mission era led to a prosperous and romantic lifestyle in

The formal dining room of the Olivas Adobe near Ventura reflects the Mission-inspired taste of yeast magnate Major "Max" Fleishman, who restored the house in 1927.

Monterey, Santa Barbara, and Los Angeles during the Mexican period. Soon the Yankee settlers transformed the adobe homesteads of the Californios and the interior styles as well.

The discovery of gold in California drastically quickened the pace of settlement of the Golden State and the creation of an eclectic home style that included traditional Hispanic elements from the mission era, oriental luxuries, and modern American furniture of English heritage. The Mission style was largely forgotten as the world fell under the spell of Victorian styles, and the astonishing boomtown of San Francisco led the way with gilded opulence. The brief interlude between the end of the mission days and the fantastic gold rush saw the decline of the missions as California's major architectural stylistic influence and the rise of a hybrid style that seemed to change from year to year. Still, the classic and enduring missions eventually provided California with its true and original building and home style.

The stately facade of the Olivas Adobe near Ventura is an excellent example of California's Territorial style, a combination of Spanish Colonial adobe construction and Greek Revival style. Raymundo Olivas built the house in 1847 and raised twenty-one children there with his wife, Theodora.

The distant image of the Alhambra is reflected in the overflowing gardens, fortresslike architecture, and decorative accents of this Mission-style house in Santa Barbara.

LITERARY CHAMPIONS ··· By the 1880s, American settlers had begun to "civilize" most parts of the West. San Francisco had emerged from a sleepy Spanish mission vil-

lage to a wild and raucous boom-town to a sophisticated world port-of-call. Wealthy Santa Fe residents covered up their humble adobe houses with Victorian rugs, lace, curtains, bric-a-brac, and Eastlake furniture. Tucson was still a small Mexican-frontier adobe village, a favorite target of Apache raids. ··· Dime-store novels and such national magazines as *Harper's Weekly* published fantastic stories of western legends, including Billy the Kid, Crazy Horse, and General George Armstrong Custer, for an insatiable American audience.

Charles Fletcher Lummis's house, called "El Alisal," was constructed of boulders gathered from the nearby Arroyo Seco. Historian James Birkit described the house as a "neo-Mission mystical pot-pourri" that combined Mexican, Pueblo, Mission Indian, and New England influences.

Improbable western stories embellished by imaginative writers provided Americans with a major form of popular entertainment in the decades before motion pictures appeared. Perhaps it was inevitable, then, that the revival of the Mission style was spearheaded by writers.

Renewed interest in the Mission style corresponded with the amazing growth of southern California in the 1880s. Railroad tracks of the Atchison, Topeka, and Santa Fe (A.T. & S.F.) finally reached San Diego in 1883 and Los Angeles in 1885. San Diego's population grew from 5,000 in 1884 to 32,000 in 1888. Although dwarfed by San Francisco's 300,000 residents, within a generation both San Diego and Los Angeles began to rival the Bay City.

Helen Hunt Jackson arrived in southern California in 1882 to report on the condition of California Indians for the United States government. While on the Cahuilla Indian Reservation, south of Riverside near Hemet, Jackson heard a tragic story of doomed Indian lovers who became the inspiration for her novel *Ramona*, published in 1884. Generously spiced with scenes of southern California and the mission lifestyle, *Ramona* skillfully plucked the heartstrings of a Victorian-era audience and zoomed to the top of the bestseller lists. Almost simultaneously, Jackson published an illustrated book of essays titled *Glimpses of California and the Missions* in 1883, which began to plead the case for the preservation of the missions.

California soon gained further notoriety, thanks to a publicity stunt by a wiry young Harvard man who "tramped across the continent" from September 1, 1884, to February 1, 1885. Charles Fletcher Lummis, at the age of twenty-five, contracted with Colonel Harrison Gray Otis, publisher of the *Los Angeles Times*, to walk across the United States from Cincinnati to Los Angeles and produce a weekly

Helen Hunt Jackson's bestselling book *Ramona*, published in 1884, evoked the Mission era of early California. Its success inspired a major outdoor "Ramona" pageant in Hemet, California, still celebrated today. Shown is the 1932 pageant program.

HELEN HUNT JACKSON
MISSION MASTER

...

Few writers enjoy profound influence; fewer still witness the effects of their phrases while still living. Helen Hunt Jackson, a New Englander, ventured out to southern California in the early 1880s to report on the condition of native California Indians for the Department of the Interior. Culturally sensitive and sympathetic, Jackson wrote the first novel about southern California, a syrupy melodrama titled *Ramona*, which would forever change the face of California architecture.

Ramona's appearance in 1884 followed Jackson's nonfiction account of the missions, handsomely illustrated by Canadian artist Henry Sandham, called *California and the Missions*. *Ramona*'s astounding popularity, comparable to *Uncle Tom's Cabin* and *Gone With the Wind*, spread the intoxicating allure of California and the mission churches nationwide.

The evocative literary foundation of the Mission Revival movement thus produced a somewhat theatrical movie-set architecture during the early years, which matured in time with more serious and scholarly design approaches. In Jackson's time, the California missions were in serious disrepair. Henry Sandham's wonderful drawings of the missions, California Indians, and old Los Angeles, are a fascinating record of the long-lost lifestyle that inspired Helen Hunt Jackson and that many still seek to recapture in one form or another.

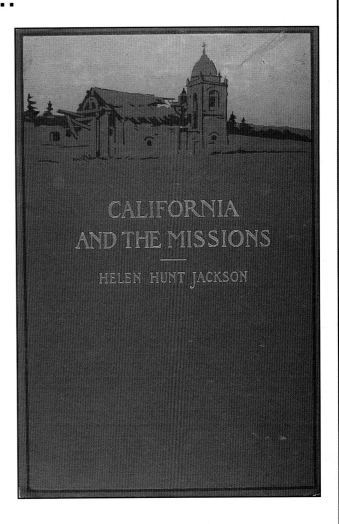

A book cover from the 1903 edition of Helen Hunt Jackson's *California and the Missions* displays artist Henry Sandham's sensitive and inspiring drawings of the neglected missions as they appeared a century ago.

column about his experiences. Lummis's descriptions of Denver, the Rocky Mountains, Santa Fe, Pueblo Indians, Navajo country, the Grand Canyon, and other wonders captivated a national audience. By the end of the decade, Lummis was a reporter for the *Los Angeles Times*, espousing a return to California's true original style of architecture—the missions.

By 1895, the Landmarks Club of California was formally incorporated with the goal of preserving the missions. Lummis was elected the club's first president. At his dramatic self-built home called "El Alisal" in east Los Angeles near Pasadena, Lummis invited leading artistic and literary personalities for lively discussions on California and Southwest culture. With the influence of such intellectuals as painter Maynard Dixon, archaeologist Adolph Bandelier, and writer Eugene Manlove Rhodes, Lummis formed an inspired vision of the Mission style as paramount to the success of California.

Historian James W. Birkit has interpreted Lummis's remarkable career in two unpublished essays: "Southwest Imagery: A Mugwump Romance" and "The Neo-Mission Cult in Southern California, 1884–1914." In the latter essay, Birkit

The interior of Charles Lummis's house El Alisal displays photographs and artifacts collected from Lummis's adventures in the Southwest and South America. The interesting buffet cabinet is a blend of Craftsman and New Mexican styles.

Artist Henry Sandham renders the deteriorating condition of San Luis Rey Mission in elegiac tones in this engraving that was originally published in the 1883 Helen Hunt Jackson book *California and the Missions*.

describes "El Alisal" as a "combination of Mexican, Pueblo Indian, Mission Indian, and New England architecture," a perfect example of the "mystical potpourri which might be called the Neo-Mission."

In its earliest manifestations, the Mission Revival style was not only an effort to preserve crumbling Spanish missions but coincided with a general feeling of ennui among many creative people for European culture and urban lifestyle. The architectural heritage of the missions, with references to Moorish and Native American cultures, appealed to many people in the West who were tired of Victorian fussiness. The attraction of the "mystical potpourri" of the new Mission style was expressed in countless houses and commercial buildings across the United States, mostly in the West, for nearly fifty years after Helen Hunt Jackson and Charles F. Lummis first sang its praises.

A NEW CALIFORNIA • • • At the turn of the century, from 1890 to 1910, a new California emerged from Helen Hunt Jackson's romanticism, Charles Lummis's preaching and preservation, and a skyrocketing economy. While the Mission Revival style was the rage of the day, it was by no means the only new style being produced on the West Coast.

Much of American architecture, however, was overwhelmed by the impressive display of classical architecture, heavily influenced by the French Beaux-Arts school, on display at Chicago's World Columbian Exposition of 1893. While many people were swayed by the grandeur of McKim, Mead, and White's master plan and Louis Sullivan's dazzling Transportation Building, the California Building by architect A. Page Brown unveiled the first major expression of the Mission Revival style—a concoction of Moorish, Mission, and Romanesque elements borrowed from the design portfolio of architect Henry Hobson Richardson.

Mission-style champion Charles Lummis's house in Los Angeles is a romantic concoction of historical Southwestern architectural forms, including this tower that resembles a New Mexican torréon, or defensive tower.

CHARLES FLETCHER LUMMIS
MISSION MASTER

∎ ∎ ∎

On February 1, 1885, a twenty-six-year-old man arrived in Los Angeles with much fanfare after having walked across most of the United States from Ohio. Charles Fletcher Lummis thus began a remarkable career promoting and preserving southwestern culture, distinguishing himself as the father of the modern Mission style.

Lummis's relentless talents embraced the fields of exploration, ethnology, linguistics, photography, journalism, library and curatorial science, folklore, musicology, conservation, and historic preservation. Lummis's tenure in Los Angeles from 1885 until his death in 1928 literally defined the Mission Revival era, which he championed with his famous declaration that "the California missions are worth more than money. They are a greater asset to southern California than our oil, our oranges, and even our climate."

As a city editor with the *Los Angeles Times* between 1885 and 1887, Lummis promoted the development of a California architectural style based upon the examples of the Spanish missions. The California pavilion at the 1893 Columbian World Exposition in Chicago by architect A. Page Brown was one of the first responses to Lummis's exhortations.

More than just a booster, Lummis encouraged a multicultural and scholarly approach to the Mission style, avidly collecting artifacts from his travels to New Mexico and Peru and photographing everything he saw, producing an amazing archive of over five thousand glass-plate negatives. In his love and appreciation of southwestern culture as a basis for a Mission lifestyle, Lummis is both the contrast and complement to the Mission style often associated with the Stickley family.

Among Lummis's many accomplishments, his role in founding the Southwest Museum in Los Angeles from 1907 to 1914 and his leadership of the Landmarks Club after 1897 are among his finest. One of America's earliest and most significant historic preservation organizations, the Landmarks Club, was instrumental in the emergency preservation of missions at San Diego, San Juan Capistrano, San Fernando, and the Asistencia of Pala.

Among the most fascinating Lummis monuments is his own house of El Alisal, named for the sycamore trees on its site on the Arroyo Seco just west of Pasadena. Operating as a salon des artistes in Los Angeles, the Lummis home holds a treasure trove of exotic trophies and examples of his unique interpretation of Mission style. Said to be a collaboration of Lummis and painter Maynard Dixon, the cabinets and hardware of El Alisal somehow fuse the ethereal spirit of Pueblo design with the permanence of Old Spain.

Named for sycamore trees it surrounds, Charles Lummis's Los Angeles home, El Alisal, is an inspired eclectic fantasy of Mission, Pueblo, and Spanish Colonial architecture.

The Mission Revival style was ideally suited to the dual demands of a land and real estate boom in southern California and also California's emergence as a major national tourism destination. The long and linear profiles of the Mission style were easily adapted by the railroad industry as depots and hotels. The A.T. & S.F. and the Southern Pacific quickly adopted the Mission style as their official architectural image, and within a decade Mission-style buildings followed the railroad tracks from Los Angeles and San Diego to Kansas City.

The railroads also brought to California a new generation of architectural talent, which transformed and redefined the region's architecture during the Mission Revival era. Among these newcomers were Bernard Maybeck, who arrived in San Francisco in 1888, Charles and Henry Greene, and Irving Gill, who all arrived in southern California in 1893.

Mission Revival architecture, above all, was an eclectic expression during its heyday, presenting different stylistic preferences and construction techniques. Architects sought prototypes in the rounded arches of medieval Spain and France, in the minaret towers of North Africa, in the intricate decor of the Alhambra, in the exuberant baroque facades of Mexico, and finally, in the pleasing pure geometry of the missions themselves. Engineers and architects developed a construction technique of applying rough stucco to metal lath strips and concrete as an effective and economical way to simulate the massive adobe construction.

Among the earliest monuments of the Mission Revival style is the great university created by Leland and Jane Stanford to commemorate their son's death in 1884. The Stanfords desired a distinctive Californian architecture for the school, featuring red tile roofs, courtyards, and sweeping arcaded verandas. Though dominated by the stone masonry and Romanesque personality championed by H. H.

California's architectural fascination with its Spanish heritage produced a spectacular display at San Diego's Pacific Panama Exposition of 1915. The California State Building draws inspiration from the high Mexican baroque style also known as Churrigueresque.

IRVING GILL
MISSION MASTER
...

One of the intriguing dates in the saga of the Mission style is 1893, the year that architects Irving Gill and Charles and Henry Greene arrived in Southern California. In San Diego, Irving Gill developed a streamlined and modern interpretation of Mission architecture, and in Pasadena, the Greenes pushed the Craftsman ideal to its logical limit. Gill revolutionized the use of concrete in home construction, and the Greenes revolutionized the use of wood. Between the examples of Gill and the Greenes, southern California would develop unique and affordable houses known as bungalows.

Irving Gill's design philosophy was perhaps as simple and straightforward as the appearance of his buildings. Gill expressed a "passion for [ornamental] elimination" and a respect for the simple geometry of "cube, line, circle, and arch" he found in the Spanish Missions of California. But Gill came around slowly, producing his best work after the inventive and experimental first phases of the Mission Revival from the 1890s to the early 1900s.

Gill studied the avant-garde writings and projects of early European modernists, whose demands for pure form matched his own sensibilities. He followed the dramatic advances in concrete technology of his day, in contrast to the Greenes' romantic evocation of ancient Japanese wood joinery, mastering the tilt-slab construction technique whereby entire walls and arcades of concrete were poured in place, hardened, then tilted into position.

In numerous San Diego and Los Angeles projects between 1907 and 1920, Irving Gill transformed the Mission style from a charming historical hybrid to a progressive expression of serene simplicity. The elegance and precision of his planar forms still appear fresh, and Gill is much admired by many designers.

In his interior design, Gill also followed his instinct for simplification, preferring clean white walls, minimally designed cabinets and wall paneling, and rich wooden surfaces. The great architectural historian Henry-Russel Hitchcock pointed out that Gill's interiors were actually more Japanese in spirit and feeling than those of the Greenes. Irving Gill was that rare talent who could fuse ancient Mission forms, a Zen design attitude, and revolutionary concrete technology to produce an architecture of lasting appeal.

The Morgan House in Hollywood, designed by Irving Gill, incorporates the streamlined Mission forms and advanced concrete construction that Gill pioneered.

Richardson, the foremost medievalist of the day, the original Stanford University buildings built between 1887 and 1891 incorporated the Mission style required by the Stanfords.

In other major examples, the Mission Revival style displayed overtly Moorish references in Pasadena's Hotel Green (1898), and a complete menu of Mediterranean, Hispanic, and fantasy Mission-style forms in the Mission Inn at Riverside (1902). Charles Lummis's remarkable home, built from 1895 to 1910 combined some Mission forms with a rustic Arts and Crafts-style vernacular construction using river boulders.

After the initial experimental years of the Mission Revival, San Diego architect Irving Gill emerged with a surprisingly pure and modern interpretation of the Hispanic forms. By 1910, European modernism and a fascination with streamlined machines began to radically transform architecture. "Less is more" became the

The interior of Greene and Greene's Irwin House in Pasadena was a substantial expansion in 1907 of a house they designed for Katherine M. Duncan in 1900. The interior is a straightforward Craftsman design with Japanese architecture in the generous, flowing eaves and complex cross-timbering.

Charles and Henry Greene mastered the expressive and structural possibilities of wood in both interior and exterior uses. The garden porch facade of the Irwin House clearly displays the Greenes' growing fascination with Japanese architecture.

San Diego architect Irving Gill avidly followed the latest developments in modern European design, adopting a less-is-more philosophy for his own designs. The 1915 kitchen of the McMakin House utilizes prefabricated cabinets and still appears strikingly contemporary.

credo of many designers, who gleefully stripped away ornament and historical references from their buildings.

Gill recognized the inherent pure geometry of the missions, evident in arcades, domes, and towers. Gill's buildings reduced the Mission style to pure form and mass, cleanly articulated in concrete and rendered in the white and neutral tones of the original missions. In a series of landmark buildings, including the 1909 Christian Science Church of San Diego, the 1910 Lewis Courts of Sierra Madre, the 1913 La Jolla Women's Club, and the 1916 Dodge House in Los Angeles, Irving Gill produced a twentieth-century version of the Mission style, a refined and elegant modernism that still influences today's designers.

By 1920, Mission-style homes pervaded southern California and the Southwest. The popularity of builders' magazines such as *The Craftsman* spread the appeal of

A bedroom in the McMakin House pays homage to the streamlined design attitude of architect Irving Gill. The simple but precise craftsmanship of the architecture and furniture are hallmarks of Gill's design.

the Mission aesthetic to a national audience, and some Mission-style homes appeared in suburbs in nearly all parts of America.

Typical elements of Mission Revival houses included curvilinear or stepped parapets, sometimes adorned with a quatrefoil or arched window, an arcaded entry porch, perhaps a bell tower, and the signature tile roof with wide overhanging eaves. In most examples, walls were stuccoed smooth and painted in white or light, neutral colors. Mission Revival houses and commercial buildings were also built in red or yellow brick. Mission homes freely borrowed architectural elements and influences from other popular American styles of the era, including Craftsman bungalows and the Prairie style.

In New Mexico and southern Colorado, architects Isaac Hamilton Rapp and his brother Charles experimented with a variety of turn-of-the-century styles, including the Mission Revival, Richardsonian Romanesque, and World's Fair Classic. The Rapp firm was hired by the New Mexico Territory to produce a Mission-style pavilion for the Louisiana Purchase Centennial Exposition of 1904 in St. Louis. This Mission example was followed by a house for Senator Bronson Cutting in Santa Fe (1910) and the Santa Fe Elks Club (1912). Other regional architects, such as Trost

Hodgin Hall on the campus of the University of New Mexico in Albuquerque is an excellent example of the early period of the Pueblo Revival style that fused Pueblo architectural forms with modernist refinements such as Art Deco.

Of all major California architects working with the Mission
style after 1910, Irving Gill was
most sympathetic to the modern
European designers. A patio he
designed for the Morgan House
anticipates the refinements of
the International style that swept
the world after 1930.

and Trost of El Paso, were also producing examples of the Mission style in West Texas and southern Arizona.

By 1915, however, leading artists, writers, and intellectuals in Santa Fe and Taos were clamoring for a return to the old Pueblo and Spanish architecture of New Mexico. Isaac Hamilton Rapp synthesized New Mexico mission facades in a remarkable pavilion at the 1915 Pacific Panama Exposition in San Diego. Thus, a major significant variation of the Mission Revival movement—the Pueblo Revival style—was launched. This style has also become know as the Santa Fe style.

THE PACIFIC PANAMA EXPOSITION AND ITS AFTERMATH ••• Despite the

popularity of the Mission Revival style in California and the Southwest, the missions themselves could not fully express the spectrum of Hispanic architecture or experience in the Americas. The Mission Revival, in fact, unleashed a dynamic and exciting rediscovery of the Spanish Colonial heritage of the Southwest, which had been neglected for at least fifty years after the Mexican War. The major currents of the Spanish Renaissance of the Southwest converged at San

Diego's 1915 Pacific Panama Exposition, creating a synergy that deeply influenced American architecture for the next two decades.

San Diego's Balboa Park saw the emergence of the Spanish Colonial Revival and the Pueblo Revival of New Mexico. Under the influence of architect Bertram Goodhue, the richly ornamented Mexican and Latin American churches of the Spanish Colonial era (1500–1850) were chosen as appropriate models for the exposition's buildings.

San Diego Exposition officials reasoned that the Franciscans and Jesuits of the northern Mexican frontier (now the American Southwest) would have built elaborate Mission churches in the Mexican style if they had had the tools and resources to do so. Therefore, in theory and spiritual affinity, the Mexican missions became the inspiration for the next wave of Spanish style in the United States—the Spanish Colonial Revival. Meanwhile, the remarkable New Mexico pavilion, itself

Because of its overwhelming Victorian heritage and longing for Old World (English and French) respectability, San Francisco did not immediately become engulfed in the Mission mania of southern California. By 1910, however, Mission Revival and Spanish Colonial Revival homes began to dot the hillsides of the Bay City.

The California Mission style was quickly adopted by the Santa Fe Railroad for depots, hotels, and other associated buildings after 1895. The railroad depot in Raton, New Mexico, still includes an arcaded breezeway, curvilinear parapet, and impressive tower built nearly a century ago.

a synthesis of New Mexico mission elements inspired the Pueblo Revival, still a powerful aesthetic throughout the region.

More romantic in approach than scholarly, the Spanish Colonial Revival offered a glamorous variation of the Mission style with more overt stylistic and cultural overtones of Spanish glory and the mystique of the Mediterranean. It was an Old World concoction that appealed to the wealthy new classes of industrialists, agricultural barons, movie stars, and high-stake developers flocking to the suddenly attainable paradises of California and Florida.

The Spanish Colonial Revival appeared at the right time and in the right places for the right people. Santa Barbara recreated itself after 1920 in a brilliant Spanish Colonial theme. Ostentatious Spanish Colonial or "Mediterranean" mansions studded the hillsides of Hollywood, Beverly Hills, Pasadena, and Santa Monica. In Florida, entire communities were designed with a quasi-Spanish personality to lure rich city exiles, retirees, and sun worshipers to Boca Raton, Coral Gables, Palm Beach, and Miami Beach.

By the Roaring Twenties, the humble and pure Mission forms of the Franciscan padres were clothed in the royal trappings of a style that borrowed from heavily

Mission Revival homes of the 1920s and 1930s, such as this Santa Monica hacienda, line the blocks of some of Los Angeles's most fashionable neighborhoods.

carved Mexican baroque Churrigueresque, Spanish and Italian Renaissance, Spanish Gothic, Moorish, and Byzantine sources. The Spanish Colonial Revival built upon the earlier success of the Mission Revival and introduced Spanish style to an even-greater national audience.

Mission Revival, Spanish Colonial Revival, and Pueblo Revival architecture inspired other fascinating fads such as Pueblo Deco, a mixture of Pueblo massing and Art Deco ornamentation, and the Mayan Revival. To many people, however, the word mission has come to symbolize and express the resurgence of Spain's architectural legacy in the United States that dominated the Southwest from 1890 to 1930.

The Great Depression and World War II ended America's long flirtation with the memory of the Franciscans and the mirage of Alhambra looming far off beyond the marshlands of Louisiana and the coral shores of Florida. The austere perfection of the International style, incorporating metal casement windows, glass block, machine metal and chrome, and flat, white walls mesmerized a post-World War II America wishing to look forward to an industrial future. In spirit, attitude, and aesthetics, the International style was the antithesis of the missions.

Recently reopened after a spec-
■ tacular refurbishing, the Mission-
■ style Beverly Hills Hotel symbol-
■ izes the romance and glamour of
a bygone era.

The large Mission-style furniture with leather upholstery was quickly dis-
carded and forgotten in favor of sleek chrome and leather designs by Mies van der
Rohe, Charles Eames, and Alvar Aalto. Nearly fifty years passed before Mission
style found a new audience in the 1980s.

The Mission Revival left in its wake not only a remarkable collection of preserved Spanish Mission complexes from California to Texas but also a sense of
regional identity, which had almost been obliterated by the onslaught of Victoriana
in the West. Furthermore, the Mission Revival exposed many Americans to a sense
of unfamiliar and exotic beauty, and therein was the heart of its appeal. Even today,
the great monuments of the Mission Revival era invite poetic and nostalgic
descriptions as if the stage were set for a tragic love story.

The Mission Revival style flourished at the same time that Victorian influence was losing its hold on home design and notions of "modern" taste. As the success of wave after wave of Victorian historical fashions swept the English and American landscapes from 1850 to 1890, the seeds of profound change were

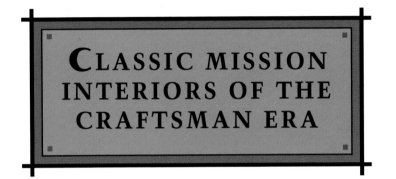

CLASSIC MISSION INTERIORS OF THE CRAFTSMAN ERA

being sown in England. The Arts and Crafts movement of England, championed by architect Augustus Pugin, writer John Ruskin, and designer William Morris, established its philosophical roots from 1840 to 1870 and finally burst into full-scale production by 1880. The ideals and aesthetic of the Craftsman movement popular in England and the eastern United States seemed to complement the Mission tradition as it was being reinterpreted

Strong Prairie-style design is evident in Frank Lloyd Wright's famous interior design for Alice Barnsdall's "Hollyhock House," built from 1917 to 1920 in Los Angeles.

by architects, writers, and designers in the West. At the heart of the Craftsman philosophy were the lofty values of honest craftsmanship, natural materials, simple and pure design, and harmonious family life. These are values that appealed to many people in the 1890s and resound in the strife-ridden 1990s.

Because of the coincidence of the Mission Revival and the Craftsman movement, Mission and Craftsman furnishings are nearly synonymous in usage and meaning. It is perhaps useful to define Mission-style furniture as the Western Craftsman style or vice-versa. In fact, several prominent furniture companies such as Roycroft and Stickley produced signature Craftsman lines, made minor or no modifications and marketed nearly identical "Mission" lines. The rage for the Mission style in California, the Southwest, and nationwide demanded effective Mission marketing. The general public knew Craftsman products as "Mission" style.

While major Craftsman furniture companies, largely based in the Midwest and East, dominated the national industry from 1900 to 1920, several western designers

The impressive mansion designed by Frank Lloyd Wright for millionaire oil heiress Alice Barnsdall in East Hollywood has become known as the "Hollyhock House" for its stylized hollyhock ornamentation motifs. Built between 1917 and 1920, the Barnsdall house also expressed Wright's growing fascination with pre-Columbian architecture, as seen in the Mayan temple references.

The interiors of the Hollyhock House are among Frank Lloyd Wright's finest, displaying a complete integration of architecture, furniture, textiles, and fine art. The famous "hollyhock" cast-concrete design icon of the house is seen in the central structural column.

In 1906, the Greene brothers enlarged one of their earlier houses—the Duncan House in Pasadena—to accommodate the family of Theodore M. Irwin. The resulting interior spaces were enlarged and streamlined. The Irwin House family room contains the essential comforts of later bungalow dens, including built-in bookshelves, window nook, and massive central fireplace.

produced distinctive furniture and accessories that incorporated oriental or Spanish elements. The presence in California and the Southwest of design geniuses such as Greene and Greene and Frank Lloyd Wright during the Mission Revival era helped shape an eclectic and dynamic furniture movement rather than a static Mission style with no innovation.

In fact, southwestern and California furniture design during the Mission Revival (and later, Spanish Colonial Revival era) borrowed freely from the Craftsman, Hispanic, and, to a limited degree, Japanese traditions. Interiors were likely to contain Craftsman pieces alongside Spanish baroque and Spanish colonial pieces, especially in New Mexico.

CRAFTSMAN IDEALS ▪▪▪ In England, designer William Morris championed an Arts and Crafts movement with the lofty goals of reforming art and society. Influenced by the Gothic Revival architecture of Augustus Pugin and the medieval romanticism of John Ruskin, Morris envisioned a democratic society where honest

In one of Greene and Greene's "ultimate bungalows," the David B. Gamble House of 1908 in Pasadena, bedrooms opened onto "sleeping porches." Here, the popular notion that wicker furniture is a natural complement to Craftsman and Mission furniture is reinforced. This bedroom suite of wicker furniture was specially designed by Charles S. Greene for the Gamble House.

work, superior handcraftsmanship, pure and simple design, and harmonious family life replaced the social injustices of the Industrial Revolution. Overworked and frivolous design of the Victorians would be transcended by refined arts and crafts produced by hand rather than machine, using high-quality natural materials and incorporating design that respected nature's own colors, patterns, and textures.

Ironically, Morris's own career and commissions were supported by England's aristocracy and wealthy upper classes. His ideas and art only superficially reached the masses in Europe, whom he wished to reform. The Arts and Crafts movement would, however, find a new life in the United States after Morris's death in 1896.

By 1899, popular American design magazines such as *House Beautiful* began to publish the work of Frank Lloyd Wright, whose Prairie home designs and furniture freely incorporated Craftsman ideals. About the same time, Gustav Stickley began to manufacture Craftsman furniture at his studio, The Craftsman Workshops, in Eastwood, New York. In 1901,

A cozy breakfast corner is created in a Utah bungalow by combining a handsome English Arts and Crafts sideboard with a classic Stickley Brothers trestle table and side chairs.

Stickley published the first issue of his successful magazine, *The Craftsman*, which introduced and educated thousands of readers in the Craftsman philosophy until its demise in 1916. These fifteen years defined the height of popularity of the Craftsman style, or as it was better known by the public, "Mission" style.

The new Craftsman movement struck a powerful chord in the American psyche. On the eastern seaboard, the simplified furniture reminded Americans of American Colonial classic designs such as the Windsor chair. In the West, the Mission furniture obviously evoked the Spanish Colonial tradition and the region's rediscovery of its Spanish and Mission heritage.

Although the Craftsman style never gained the popular favor of the American upper classes, who preferred English baroque and Georgian furniture in their town houses, it proved highly popular for most middle-class families. Ironically, the true

Traci and Mikel Covey's bungalow in Utah captures the essence
of the western Craftsman style, incorporating an eclectic and
refined approach. English Arts and Crafts dining chairs recall the
influence of Scottish designer Charles Rennie Mackintosh, and
the sideboard by the Stickley Brothers is a fine display cabinet
for a striking collection of Craftsman ceramics.

By the mid-1920s in Los Angeles, Frank Lloyd Wright began to experiment with cast-concrete block construction. The Millard House of 1923 in Pasadena was the first of these block houses. Called "La Miniatura," the Millard House interior shows a vertical accommodation to the confined site, a contrast to Wright's earlier "Prairie" earth-hugging designs.

Sited at the edge of a ravine in Pasadena, Frank Lloyd Wright's "La Miniatura" house of 1923 was designed to evoke the image of a Mayan temple emerging from the jungle.

"handcraftsmanship" espoused by Morris and Gustav Stickley was mass-manufactured in the United States and sold to the common man. Only prosperous or wealthy clients could afford the true Craftsman or Mission style produced by Frank Lloyd Wright, Greene and Greene, Stickley, Roycroft, Harvey Ellis, or other famous designers.

It was also ironic that in spite of its roots in medieval craftsmanship, Mission furniture designs were surprisingly streamlined, refined, and modern. Few Craftsman designs boasted any carving or overt historical references. The straightforward simplicity of Craftsman furniture anticipated and influenced the work of future modernist furniture designers such as Alvar Aalto and Charles Eames.

THE GREAT DESIGNERS • • • In the East and Midwest, Craftsman designs by the Stickley brothers (Gustav, Leopold, and John George) and Prairie-style-pioneered architecture and furnishings by Frank Lloyd Wright were governed by both rectilinear and horizontal lines. Chairs, bookcases, and clocks provided dramatic vertical accents; tables were long and low slung; and cabinets provided the happy medium.

While Stickley offered Craftsman house designs, published in *The Craftsman*, that were often influenced by English medieval cottages, Chicago's Prairie-school architects sought more integrated architectural solutions. Desiring to visually unite the interiors and exteriors of houses, Prairie architects also sought to create homes that appeared rooted in the land or Prairie, itself.

Led by Frank Lloyd Wright, George Grant Elmslie, and George Washington Maher, the Prairie school produced boldly creative furniture and accessories to complement their architecture. Faithful to the Craftsman aesthetic of natural materials, Prairie furniture achieved a dramatic sculptural unity, not unlike the

An intimate inglenook in the
Covey bungalow in Utah is dominated by an impressive river-rock
hearth and a settle by Gustav
Stickley.

The adjoining dining and living rooms of the Bible residence in Los Angeles reflect a conservative and traditional approach to the furnishing of a typical western bungalow home. Craftsman-era furniture, textiles, and ceramics harmonize effortlessly.

Prairie school architecture itself. Next to the sometimes-cumbersome Stickley examples, Prairie-school furniture appears light and aerodynamic.

In the West, however, high-style Craftsman furniture and interiors acquired an exotic personality mostly unknown in the Midwest and East. California and south-western designers fused the Craftsman aesthetic with Spanish, Japanese, and Native American influences to create the true "Mission" style.

The buildings and homes of the Mission Revival provided a ready market for the new Craftsman furniture. Most western architects sought not to completely integrate Mission furniture with their interior designs but rather to complement the Spanish or Mission architecture. Native American crafts, including Pueblo pottery, Navajo rugs, and Apache baskets, accented many Mission homes. As examples of pure craft and design, the Indian crafts were highly praised and desired for Mission-style interiors.

Perhaps the spirit of the California Mission style was best exemplified by

The great entrance hall of the David B. Gamble House in Pasadena by Greene and Greene provides the ultimate synthesis of Craftsman-era architecture and interior design. The sublime qualities of this space have been poetically described by architectural historian Reyner Banham: *"At sunup the wood itself is bathed in Tiffany tones from the broad swatches of gold and green light that pour through those doors and fall directly upon the paneling . . . that rather formal central space . . . is transformed . . . into something so perfectly 'cliche'—Aladdin's cave or a sacred grove—then you know it must be a great work of art . . ."* (Randell Makinson, <u>Greene & Greene.</u> [Layton, Utah: Gibbs Smith, Publisher, 1977], 21.)

Charles F. Lummis's El Alisal named for the great sycamore tree it surrounded. A true eclectic fantasy constructed of large boulders from the nearby Arroyo Seco, El Alisal is part hacienda and part bungalow, and is crowned by a pseudo-Mission gable complete with a bell. The interiors, designed with the help of the great painter Maynard Dixon, are inspired by both the Craftsman and New Mexican traditions. Lummis's own collection of Native American artifacts, collected from the Southwest, Mexico, and South America, give El Alisal an aura of museum-like authenticity.

For many, the California Craftsman movement is epitomized by the remarkable architecture and interior design of brothers Charles S. and Henry Greene. Credited with developing the trademark American house of the pre-World War II era—the bungalow—the Greene brothers displayed a keen understanding of the integration of architecture, arts, and crafts—the true goal of the Craftsman movement.

In their greatest houses, such as the David B. Gamble house (1908) and the R.

Built in 1908 at a cost of fifty thousand dollars (when medium-sized schools cost half that much), the David B. Gamble House is considered by many to be among the most influential American houses of the twentieth century. The complex joinery and roofs inspired by Japanese architecture have inspired comparisons of the Gamble House to a great ship.

Though inspired by Japanese architecture, the design of Greene and Greene produced a uniquely Californian expression of the Craftsman ideal: sumptuous, exotic, and timeless. As described by historian Reyner Banham, *". . . in the rounding and shaping of the woodwork . . . the Japanese influence is most commonly thought to be seen, but . . . it is not Japanese carpentry that is imitated but something more like the rounding and polishing in Netsuke, or the conventions for light and mist in the prints of Hokusai and Hiroshige."*

R. Blacker house (1907), both in Pasadena, the Greenes designed mostly everything. Their refined touch can be seen in furniture, built-in cabinets, lighting, stained glass, picture frames, hardware, and other interior details.

Though their architecture cannot be described as Mission Revival, the Greene brothers' style was surprisingly international in its influences, and included English cottages, Japanese construction and joinery, and the wooden architectures of southern Germany, Switzerland, and Scandinavia. Their great achievement was to produce a uniquely Californian architecture out of these varied styles.

The Greenes fully appreciated the Spanish Mission heritage of California, though they recognized the sometimes show-biz eccentricities of Golden State architecture. In his essay on Charles and Henry Greene published in *California Design 1910* (Gibbs Smith, Publisher, 1989 ed.), Randell Makinson quotes Charles Greene's observation in 1905 that California architecture was ". . . the union of a

In the furniture and interior design of the Gamble House, Greene and Greene refined their vocabulary, avoiding excessive elaboration of their earlier works and achieving a sublime sophistication, as seen in the formal dining room.

Franciscan Mission and a Mississippi steamboat. . . ." But Charles elaborates on the Mission style in a reverent, poetic tone that balances Charles Lummis's fervent rhetoric.

■ ■ ■

The old art of California—that of the Mission fathers—is old enough to be romantic and mysterious enough, too. Study it and you will find a deeper meaning than the books tell of, or sun-dried bricks and plaster show. Then too, those old monks came from a climate not unlike this. They built after their own fashion, and their knowledge of climate and habits of life were bred in the bone. Therefore, giving heed to these necessary and effective qualities, there is good and just reason why we should study their works. . . . Simple as it is, and rude, it has something that money cannot buy or skill conciliate. It runs in every line, turns in every arch, and hangs like incense in the dim cathedral light.

■ ■ ■

The legacy of Greene and Greene still hangs heavily in the West, especially in furniture design. Charles Greene delighted in furniture projects, and his work is the undisputed standard of the western Craftsman style. Characterized by delicate, tapered lines, exquisite craftsmanship and detailing, and a love of such luxurious materials as mahogany, teak, silver, ebony, and abalone shell, Greene's furniture is perhaps the most valued and collectible of all American furniture. Charles Greene's influence is still evident in the products of major contemporary furniture companies such as Berkeley Mills of Berkeley and Santa Fe and Arroyo Design of Tucson.

In contrast to the exotic, sumptuous style of Greene and Greene, Irving Gill of San Diego produced a progressive and modern interpretation of the Mission style. Gill absorbed the lessons of classic Mission architecture, stripped the basic geometric forms to their bare essentials, reconfigured them, and thus redefined the Mission style.

Gill's interiors remained faithful to the Craftsman approach but were also streamlined and devoid of excess ornamentation. He championed the use of native

An intimate corner in Greene and
Greene's Irwin House is enhanced
by a classic Craftsman armchair
and tea table in the distinctive
inlaid style of Harvey Ellis.

California redwood in his interiors and the simple Mission furniture he sometimes conceived for his clients. While Irving Gill could not equal the timeless furniture designs of Charles Greene, his architecture and streamlined interiors provided a bridge to the future International style for western designers and the first original expression of the modern Mission style.

In the San Francisco area, Bernard Maybeck developed a unique and romantic architectural style often tempered by an appreciation for European medieval styles such as French Gothic. Maybeck's architecture avoided overt Mission-style references but respected superb craftsmanship and displays of ornamentation. Julia Morgan, best known as the architect of Hearst Castle in San Simeon, sought inspiration in the Italian and Spanish Renaissance and, like Maybeck, was fond of rich decorative surfaces in her work.

The architecture of Maybeck and Morgan reflects a significant disparity in attitude between northern and southern California during the Mission Revival period.

Craftsman-era furniture and ceramics blend effortlessly with the refined "minimal" Mission architecture of Irving Gill in the living room of the McMakin House.

While Los Angeles and San Diego were striving to reinvent themselves with reworked Mission forms, the grand old dame San Francisco was striving towards Old World respectability through the expression of Classical, Gothic, and Renaissance themes. Only grudgingly would San Francisco accept the Spanish influences of its southern rivals.

CALIFORNIA CRAFTSMEN • • • Besides Irving Gill and the Greene brothers, many other creative people in the West were absorbed in the Arts and Crafts movement. At its height, the Arts and Crafts movement was expressed in other art forms such as painting, sculpture, dance, music, and stage design. In the decorative arts, the Craftsman aesthetic was manifest in ceramics, textiles, and metalwork such as lamps, silver table settings, and other accessories.

The spirit of the years before World War I encouraged experimentation and the development of personal styles but with a firm Craftsman foundation. Furniture designers found ingenious ways to craft subtle references to oriental, Spanish, medieval, and Native American designs in their products, to name a few. Other craftsmen, especially potters and ceramicists, remained true to the Craftsman emphasis on natural designs and colors.

Several California craftsmen produced sublime works that further defined the Mission style in the West. In San Francisco, the remarkable Furniture Shop of Arthur and Lucia K. Mathews, both fine artists by persuasion and training, produced a variety of decorative, handcrafted objects of timeless beauty. Adopting the clean lines of Craftsman furniture, the Mathewses embellished their pieces with hand-painted floral scenes of oriental simplicity and hand-carved figures of medieval or mythological origins. The Furniture Shop, active from about 1900 to 1920, produced a variety of beautiful accessories for the home, such as screens, painted wooden bowls, and boxes. Of all California Craftsman studios, the Furniture Shop faithfully interpreted William Morris's advice to "have nothing in your houses which you do not know to be beautiful."

Dutchman Dirk van Erp moved to the United States in 1886 and migrated to the San Francisco area, where he established a metalsmith studio by 1908. Van Erp mastered the craft of hammered metal, achieving lustrous finishes in copper and brass. Van Erp's famous "mushroom" lamp, made of hammered and riveted copper and mica light panels, is a Mission-style standard.

California produced at least a dozen first-class ceramic studios during the Mission Revival period, including Robertson pottery, Arequipa pottery, Markham pottery, California Faience, and the Ernest Batchelder studio, to name a few. Craftsman-era pottery embodied the virtues of simple, graceful forms, function, natural rather than abstract designs, and natural glazes and pigments. Painted decoration such as in Pueblo pottery were unknown, but some vessels and tiles were carved. Above all, the Craftsman potter sought the perfection of pure form and wondrous natural glazes.

Designers of the Mission Revival era practiced integration of the arts and crafts and a refinement of design and lifestyle to their essence of harmony. Unfortunately, such noble ideals had to vie with a violent world and a fickle public. By 1915, World War I had begun to reorganize national priorities. Astonishing advances in technology, such as automobiles, motion pictures, airplanes, and other wonders, ushered in a new, fast-paced society that challenged the Craftsman philosophy. Already the virtues of machines were being touted by avant-garde groups such as the Italian Futurists. By the end of World War I, the Craftsman movement had run its course in America.

The Spanish style of California, inspired by the missions, proved to be more resilient. With the dramatic display of Spanish and Mexican colonial architecture at San Diego's Pacific Panama Exposition of 1915, the Mission Revival blended seamlessly into more complex Spanish and baroque forms. Actually, the Mission Revival period ushered in an extended era of Hispanic style in the United States, which lasted for nearly fifty years, until about 1940, and saw an amazing cross-pollenization of ideas and stylistic influences from Spain, Morocco, California, New Mexico, Texas, Florida, and other places.

Though simply articulated, the ideals of the Craftsman era, intertwined with Mission architecture, had complex effects and artistic manifestations. The pure Craftsman and Mission styles were transformed into an exciting, eclectic Spanish style with more luxurious overtones that suited the booming 1920s but still captivates many today.

Warren Hile Studio of Sierra Madre, California, produces exceptional contemporary Mission furniture in the tradition of Gustav Stickley.

The interior rooms of the Irwin House of 1907 by Greene and Greene
have been called "Japanese" because of their modular design. The Irwin
dining room exemplifies the remarkable harmony of interior and furniture design that characterizes the Greenes' "ultimate bungalows" of
1907–1910.

■ Simple virtues of study, contemplation, and appreciation of nature are at

the heart of the Craftsman and Mission lifestyles—qualities beautifully

expressed in Greene and Greene's Irwin House in Pasadena.

A CIRCLE OF TIME ··· In the century following the great Mission Revival of the 1890s, the Mission style has come full circle to embrace and express all of its components,

MISSION STYLE — TODAY AND TOMORROW

such as Moorish, Spanish, Spanish Colonial, Arts and Crafts, and even Native American influences. Discovered by a new audience of talented designers, furniture makers, and architects, the Mission style of the 1990s is evolving both multidimensionally and multiculturally. The basic core of the Mission Revival style, as developed by English and American Arts and Crafts devotees, of simple, sturdy furniture; harmonious family life; natural colors and materials; and open, flowing architecture appeals to a new generation of baby boomers seeking refuge from a

The inspired Mission style of the Brian Gibson House in Los Angeles (designed by Michael Anderson) includes an impressive array of ethnic textiles, Santa Fe-style painted furniture, wrought iron, and great modern art.

frenzied and technology-driven society.

After the glamorous years of the Mission Revival period in California, when marquee neighborhoods in Hollywood, Pasadena, and Santa Monica were rising out of the foothills of Los Angeles, the long arm of European Modernism swept aside most things western and handmade. For at least fifty years, from the Great Depression until the Gulf War, the Mission style languished in obscurity, appreciated by a small but devoted following of collectors, bungalow home-owners, and fine-furniture craftsmen.

Following upon the sensational popular success of the Santa Fe- and Cowboy-style design booms of the 1980s, it was inevitable that the Mission style would be rediscovered. A growing mass migration westward in the 1990s, perhaps unprecedented since the Santa Fe and Oregon Trails and the mining booms of the nineteenth century, has breathed new life into many small desert and mountain towns and decaying inner-city neighborhoods in western cities. Consequently, the forsaken Mission Revival cottages and California bungalows across the West and Midwest are now highly prized.

The contemporary Stickley collection includes the Mission Oak Dining Collection. The suite displays a china buffet cabinet with leaded-glass windows, a keyhole trestle table, and the spindle armchair, based on a 1905 Gustav Stickley design.

The year 1992 proved to be a watershed year for the Mission and Craftsman discovery. Barbara Mayer's handsome pictorial essay *In the Arts and Crafts Style* was published; *American Bungalow* magazine, devoted to the Craftsman style, was inaugurated (and is still in publication); and the Palm Springs Desert Museum offered a landmark exhibition of Craftsman furnishings and fine art collected by Alexandria and Sidney Sheldon. As a result, surging national demand for Mission/Craftsman style has fostered a wealth of new craftsmen and designers and the endorsement of major manufacturers and catalog retailers in all parts of the United States.

The legacy of the great Mission Revival masters lives on. Gustav Stickley dreamed of a democratic society nurtured by Craftsman ideals, and now computers, catalogs, and the mass mobility of American culture have helped spread Mission products everywhere. Frank Lloyd Wright acknowledged and praised the potential of machines and manufacturing, and now his manufactured furniture designs or variations are available to the average consumer in many forms.

The 1990s most resemble the spirit of the 1890s, when the Mission Revival style was being invented by experimentation, inspiration, and genius. The simple and pure forms of Mission architecture and furniture allow many new techniques of manipulation and cross-mixing with other popular styles such as Japanese, Shaker, New Mexican, Rustic, and English. Designers today have the luxury of interpreting the Mission style along purist lines, holding fast to the Craftsman ideals—or eclectic compositions—paying homage to the approach of Mission Renaissance man Charles Fletcher Lummis. Whether the choice of architecture be bungalow, cottage, adobe, penthouse, or tepee, today's Mission style can go anywhere.

Warren Hile Studio of Sierra Madre, California, features a living-room ensemble heavily influenced by traditional Stickley designs. Shown here are a Prairie-style settle, trestle coffee table, and round tea table.

INSPIRED MISSION INTERIORS ▪ ▪ ▪ Although the experimental and eclectic Mission style of the 1990s resembles the design attitude of a century ago, modern lifestyles and family behavior have changed dramatically. The Craftsman ideal of the family clustered around a fireplace, enjoying a book together while cozily seated in Morris chairs and settles seems quaint and outdated. Today's living rooms must accommodate large cabinets for televisions and stereo equipment, and the beloved bookshelves of the Mission Revival era are likely to stock videotapes, boom boxes, and other high-tech necessities.

Today's families eat and run in various patterns and frequencies, and formal meals involving the whole family—as cherished by turn-of-the-century households—are infrequent. Modern demands on living rooms, dining rooms, and kitchens have forced new flexibility and design solutions from Mission designers.

Still, certain elements and qualities of the Mission style are timeless and must be considered in any modern interpretation. Glazed or patterned tile work; impos-

Designer Roy McMakin drew upon Mission and Spanish Colonial sources for his design of actress Katey Sagal's home in Los Angeles. Instead of producing literal reproductions of period pieces, McMakin worked with carpenters to produce contemporary Mission-style furniture, such as the neo-baroque coffee table and armchair of the living room.

ing wooden furniture; finely crafted weavings and textiles by indigenous craftsmen; elegant pottery of graceful form adorned with earth colors; and pure, natural colors for walls and accents are the basics. Superbly crafted metal lamps with elaborate mica or stained-glass shades offer creative accents. Wrought-iron architectural accents in Arabesque or Spanish designs are also classic.

Students of the Mission style can find inspiration in all or any phases of the long development of the movement, from Moorish through classic Spanish, and including Spanish Colonial, Arts and Crafts, and Mission Revival. The arts and crafts of southwestern Native American tribes, notably Navajo weavings, Pueblo pottery, and Apache baskets, are also essential elements of Mission rooms. As practiced by today's leading interior designers and stylists, Mission style implies a playful, romantic, and varied (in texture, scale, and color) approach, and Craftsman style requires a pure, complementary, and somewhat scholarly touch.

Sleekly designed wrought-iron patio furniture upholstered in "Mexican serape" colors complements the classic Mission-style architecture of actress Katey Sagal's hacienda in Los Angeles.

Twentieth-century Mission style is largely a California phenomenon. By 1910, the Mission style was rather severe and stark, an effect of dark wooden furniture in white, plastered rooms. The interiors were heavily influenced by Craftsman ideals and products. In 1995, the Mission style has returned to its Spanish sources for inspiration. Seattle designer Roy McMakin, originally of Los Angeles, recently summarized his dramatic Mission-style design for Los Angeles-based actress Katey Sagal by observing, "We didn't need period furniture; we needed new furniture with an old Spanish feeling."

Perhaps the key to the new Mission style is the imagined and emotional nostalgia of the Spanish legacy tempered by modern American standards of comfort and lifestyle. Great California and southwestern designers in the Mission style speak of creating dramatic places for living. These effects are largely produced by painting and texturing carefully selected accents in strong Mediterranean colors, complementing expanses of walls rendered in luxurious earthy tones such as apricot, Naples yellow, or pale green, and selecting a combination of Old World antiques and modern, upholstered furnishings.

The eclectic but timeless appeal of Roy McMakin's design for Katey Sagal's house is apparent in this intimate secretary nook. With the exception of the personal computer, the scene evokes the carefree elegance of the 1920s when the Mission Revival was in full swing in Southern California.

Roy McMakin designed an unusual neo-Mission television cabinet for Katey Sagal's bedroom. Mission references are evident in the curious "baroque" legs of the cabinet, as well as Fiesta-ware ceramics and a wrought-iron foot table. The overstuffed chaise is a family heirloom.

Simple forms boldly colored in Moroccan hues help create an understated but refined stairway passage in Katey Sagal's Los Angeles house.

Contemporary Mission style offers an unlimited palette of accessories, furniture, colors, textiles, and materials to choose from, providing they can be associated with Spanish, Mexican, or southwestern Native American culture. Carefully selected, massive wooden furniture should anchor each room, providing the "bass notes" in the composition. Thus, a Stickley Morris chair, or a Spanish, iron, cross-brace dining table, or an antique, Mexican baroque armoire provide the beginnings of a room design.

Traditionalists may choose a more conservative, historical approach by selecting predominantly Craftsman-era products such as Stickley or Roycroft and accessorizing with Spanish, Moorish, or southwestern ceramics and textiles. A progressive and bold approach fuses strong Moroccan colors, fine Spanish antiques, luxurious American upholstered furniture, and southwestern Indian textiles and pottery. Today's Mission style is baroque and postmodern, multicultural, romantic, and adventurous.

MODERN MISSION FURNITURE ••• For

many people, Mission furniture conjures up images of solid, dark wooden furniture with leather upholstery in the simple, straightforward style of the Stickley brothers. While contemporary Mission furniture offers interesting variations on this timeless theme, other craftsmen are exploring the definition and appearance of Mission furniture. The basic Mission Revival palette of dark-stained oak, brass, or copper hardware, and leather upholstery has been greatly expanded. The major innovations in modern Mission furniture are color, carving, hybrids with other styles, and upholstery textiles.

As the oldest Spanish colony in the United States, New Mexico is a logical place to begin surveying modern Mission furniture. For Mission/Craftsman-style purists, New Mexico offers few but excellent possibilities. Randolph Laub Studio of Santa Fe is nationally recognized for its superb Craftsman line, inspired by

This unique and useful cabinet by Warren Hile Studio combines the functions of a bookcase, secretary, and sideboard. The hardware detailing and leaded-glass panels are classic Mission style in the Stickley tradition.

Designer John Kelly of Philadelphia produces a contemporary
line of Craftsman furniture with
Shaker overtones.

Arroyo Design of Tucson, Arizona, offers a complete line of Mission furniture crafted of desert mesquite. Their "California Craftsman" side chair echoes the graceful tapers of Greene and Greene original designs.

Master craftsman Gunther Worrlein of Lamy, New Mexico, has carved an exquisite bookshelf in the Pueblo Deco style with a central sunburst motif.

A dining table by Berkeley Mills
Studio of Berkeley and Santa Fe
features Oriental references tempered by Greene and Greene
styling.

Overhanging tops, arching rails,
and bowed sides are characteristic of Harvey Ellis's designs that
inspired this chest of drawers,
which is crafted of wild black
cherry and curly maple.

Berkeley Mills Studio's unique approach to Craftsman furnishings combines Japanese *tansu* cabinets in the background with generously scaled Morris chairs in the foreground.

Stickley but modeled in lighter, rounded proportions. Berkeley Mills Studio of Berkeley and Santa Fe offers a fascinating array of Craftsman furniture with Japanese (*tansu*), Greene and Greene, Shaker, Stickley, and New Mexican influences. Berkeley Mills's style and products are eclectic, superbly crafted, and sophisticated in their refinement.

New Mexico's own long tradition of furniture design is a natural complement to the Mission style. During the Mission Revival period, New Mexico furniture craftsmen evolved the "Taos bed," a variation of the classic Mission settle. Today, Southwest Spanish Craftsmen of Santa Fe, founded in 1927 and one of the West's oldest and greatest furniture companies, has a mind-boggling portfolio full of hundreds of furniture examples in Spanish provincial, Spanish baroque, Spanish Colonial, Mission Revival, Native American, and other hybrids. Some of Southwest Spanish Craftsman's newest designs fuse Mission forms and Native American ornamentation such as carved kachina masks.

Arroyo Furniture's "Mission Slat-back Chair" recalls simple Colonial chairs of the Spanish Southwest.

Many other New Mexico craftsmen are currently producing fascinating furniture pieces that reflect the current experimental climate. Bruce Peterson of Dixon has made a Frank Lloyd Wright-inspired settee of hardwood with thin willows from the Rio Grande as back panel inserts. Eric Freyer of Albuquerque ornaments a Mission desk with Pueblo cloud and lightning designs. Jim Thomas's unique carving style evokes references to Spanish, Art Nouveau, and imaginary J. R. R. Tolkien (hobbit) furniture, and therefore could fill an exciting niche in a cutting-edge Mission interior.

Nicolai Fechin, a great Russian artist, carver, and builder, produced astonishing furniture in his Taos home from 1927 to 1933. Though not clearly defined Mission style, Fechin's delightful carving technique and furniture forms were a romantic marriage of Russian folk carvings and New Mexico structure. In size, color, mass, and spirit, Fechin's great Taos furniture is a wonderful complement to the Mission

The Grand Canyon provides a spectacular backdrop for an ensemble of classic Mission furnishings offered by Utah's Sundance catalog. The set includes a Pueblo wrought-iron floor lamp with mica shade, a Morris chair recliner, and a Mission plant stand. The scene is completed by ethnic textiles, including an Indian *dhurrie* floor rug.

style. Today, an authorized Fechin line of furniture, hardware, doors, and accessories is available through Jeremy Morelli Studios of Santa Fe.

New Mexico's neighboring states of Arizona and Colorado, as well as Kansas, are home to superb craftsmen working in the Mission spirit. Arroyo Furniture Company of Tucson has manipulated traditional Craftsman, neoclassical (Biedermeier), and Spanish Colonial styles by crafting impressive pieces out of native Arizona mesquite. Greene and Greene and Stickley Morris chairs never looked better than in the warm honey glow of polished mesquite. Watson Heirlooms of Buena Vista, Colorado, boasts a dynamic and charming style that perhaps can be described as "old California." Grape clusters, Native American (Pueblo) designs, and even painted bas-relief Mexican figures ornament Watson's cabinets. Mike Livingston of Hutchinson, Kansas, is a rare master who effortlessly conjures up carved images of African, Spanish, Cowboy, and Native American

Randolph Laub of Santa Fe crafts a line of custom Craftsman furniture true to Stickley prototypes but with lighter proportions and rounded profiles. Laub's Craftsman ensemble harmonizes easily with the adobe architecture of Santa Fe.

Southwest Spanish Craftsmen is among the West's most established furniture companies, in business since 1927. Their deep portfolio includes countless designs that would enhance a Mission interior, including a New Mexican colonial table with Moorish chip carving, a Spanish provincial highboy cabinet, and a leather-upholstered Andalusian rocking chair, shown here.

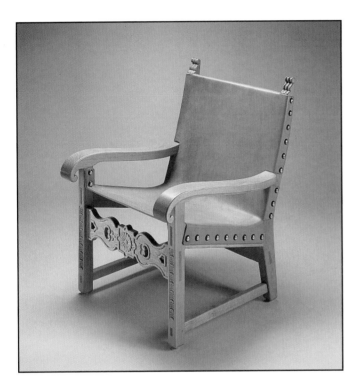

One of Southwest Spanish Craftsmen's most popular designs is the
"Andalusian Armchair," a Spanish
provincial classic.

Colorado's Watson Heirlooms
presents this dramatically carved
door, which depicts the robbery
of a stagecoach on the western
frontier.

origins to adorn his cabinets. His carved images of Catholic saints and Madonnas belong in the contemporary Mission-style vocabulary.

Many other Mission-style furniture makers employ a traditional approach, remaining faithful to Craftsman and Prairie-style examples and the Craftsman philosophy of superb craftsmanship and high-quality materials. Designers wishing to fuse Mission and Craftsman products have a wealth of resources to draw upon. Currently, the Mission and Craftsman mania has flourished in southern California, the Pacific Northwest design capital of Seattle, and in Chicago and Maine.

L. and J. G. Stickley Company of New York is the logical place to start searching for classical Mission furniture. Founded by younger brothers of Gustav Stickley, Leopold and John George, L. and J. G. Stickley has been in continuous operation for a century. Acquired in 1974 by Alfred and Aminy Audi, the Stickley Company now employs 650 craftsmen. Stickley Company has led the resurgence of Craftsman and Mission style in America by aggressive and effective marketing.

The majority of Stickley products from the Mission Oak and Cherry Collection are authentic reproductions of timeless designs by Gustav and

An impressive cabinet by Jim Thomas of Santa Fe combines Old World carving traditions with dramatic Mission-style hardware.

Leopold Stickley, Harvey Ellis, and even a few offerings from the Roycroft portfolio. While the Stickley design repertoire is classic and familiar, offering such basics as Morris chairs, trestle tables, prairie settles, and bookcases, the collection acknowledges contemporary lifestyle necessities such as entertainment-center cabinets.

Stickley is careful to innovate with its majestic Mission collection, but has expanded its selection of woods to include cherry, wild black cherry, and curly maple. The company has accepted some Shaker influence in its Duanesburg bed-

Watson Heirloom cabinet

room suite. A variety of lamps featuring stained-glass shades is also available. The L. and J. G. Stickley Company remains the standard-bearer for traditional Mission-style aesthetics.

Other regionally based furniture makers and designers offer Craftsman style furniture with a Mission spirit. Richardson Brothers Company of Sheboygan Falls, Wisconsin, makes traditional Mission furniture with some Prairie influence and attractive detailing, such as beveled-table styling and lovely tapered and curved high-back chairs. Warren Hiles Studio of Sierra Madre, California, fashions Stickley-inspired Mission furniture with slightly lighter proportions and deep, luxurious oak color. Hiles's Mission designs are enhanced by the dark "Spanish" color of the hardware.

The Mission and Craftsman styles may be accented by furniture of similar design but lighter appearance. The Naturalist furniture company of Provo, Utah, produces an Architectural Elements line that blends light western woods, such as pine and alder, with metal accents in a Craftsman-inspired styling. Progressive Shaker style, such as streamlined cabinets by John Kelly of Philadelphia, might provide an interesting alternative as a complement to the Mission style in certain situations.

A host of major American furniture manufacturers and mass-mail catalog retailers also offer select Mission furniture possibilities. The Sundance catalog of Utah sold a dynamic Mission line, featuring warm-toned oak furniture graced by luxurious leather upholstering and accented by western Mission lamps. Thomasville Furniture company offers attractive contemporary pieces based upon the great Craftsman masters (Stickley and Wright) in its American Revival line.

Today's Mission-style furniture possibilities thus span a broad spectrum, including all Spanish styles, the Craftsman era, with Shaker, Japanese, Rustic, and

A suite of Stickley furniture includes a Prairie spindle settle, Prairie spindle chair, tile-top cocktail table, Harvey Ellis armchairs, an octagonal table, and mantel clock.

John Kelly of Philadelphia produces a sleek contemporary Craftsman chair with delicate detailing
and proportioning and Shaker simplicity.

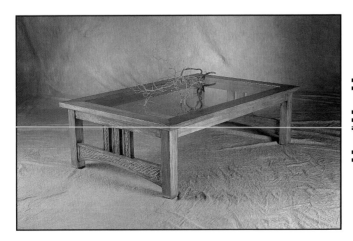

The Durango coffee table by
Ernest Thompson Furniture of
Albuquerque marries a Craftsman
spindle design with Moorish chip
carving in the New Mexican
manner.

Native American included as flourishes and inspired accents. By definition, Mission style requires a romantic and bold attitude.

Even Mission master Irving Gill, known for his restrained and refined architecture, upholstered Craftsman furniture in natural western cowhide!

NEO-MISSION ARCHITECTURE •••

Much of the dynamism and excitement of the new Mission style is being generated by architects and historic preservationists. Now that the Victorian boomtown mania of the West has waned (many Victorian buildings and homes have been bought and fixed up), bungalows offer a new generation of homeowners the opportunities for a dream home. The recent preservation and revitalization of Mission-style monuments such as the Hotel Green in Pasadena, the Mission Inn in Riverside, California, the Beverly Hills Hotel, and Albuquerque's La Posada Hotel have helped inspire many other Mission-style projects.

An historic Tucson home epitomizes the new Mission style, featuring a Pasadena armchair, a Mack side table, and a slatted writing desk from Arroyo Furniture's Mission collection.

The familiar components of Mission-style architecture—arcades, stucco plaster, tilework, clay tile roofs, courtyards, and fountains—have become staple design elements of new suburban developments in metropolitan cities across the West. Sometimes marketed as Mediterranean style, the new Mission style of the suburbs is often boxy and spare, occasionally missing the graceful curves and exotic overtones of previous eras.

A talented new generation of California architects is now unveiling dramatic expressions of Mission, Craftsman, and Spanish Colonial Revival buildings on the West Coast. Having absorbed the lessons of modernism and also delighting in the dazzling variety of new materials, colors, handcrafted products and other architectural basics, California architects have discovered the promise of Mission style's pure geometry—cube, arc, line, and circle—that so intrigued Irving Gill. The "Young Turks" of the Neo-Mission style include Ace Architects of Oakland, Marc Appleton & Associates of Venice, Barton Phelps of Los Angeles, Moore Ruble and

A Santa Fe salon, designed by connoisseur and author James Jareb, intro-
duces contemporary Moroccan style to the Southwest. Moroccan textiles, art, and colors endow the New Mexican interior architecture with
powerful transcendental energy.

Yudell of Santa Monica, and Rob Wellington Quigley of San Diego.

For the most part, the new Mission architects are a youthful breed of design mavericks with few preconceived notions of what the Mission style should or shouldn't be. They share a healthy respect for California's architectural heritage and the legacy of the great builders—the Franciscan friars, the Mission Revivalists, and the modernists. They share a postmodern attitude of experimentation, exaggeration, and juxtaposition of historical forms, and each has a sense of dramatic flair.

Ace Architects of Oakland is led by principals Lucia Howard and David Weingarten, who delight in their facility with historical architecture and their sense of whimsy. Ace Architects is loyal to their Bay Area design traditions, and recent projects include an exaggerated pink Spanish Colonial Revival townhouse, a Gothic-like Bernard Maybeck fantasy home in the Oakland Hills, built after the recent fire, and an inspired 1930s Ranch House revival complete with Mexican sombreros, thirties Monterey furniture, religious icons, and Navajo rugs. Ace Architects fully embodies the romantic spirit of the new Mission style.

Somewhat surprisingly, considering Los Angeles's sense of pretense, Southern California architects tend to express the formal, sophisticated, and restrained aspects of Mission style as depicted by Irving Gill, although Los Angeles interior designers have pioneered the exotic Old World Mission style of the 1990s. Marc Appleton and Associates of Venice, California, are equally skillful manipulating the Mission modernist vocabulary of Irving Gill, as in the recent Nasotir House, or the more textured forms of the Spanish Colonial Revival period. Appleton's Mission work features skillful layering of smooth-plastered wall forms punctuated artfully by wall and door openings.

Mission Inn was built during the imaginative heydays of the Mission Revival and offers many tantalizing architectural forms and details. The five-story, open-air International Rotunda, built about 1930, encloses offices, shops, and suites around a magnificent spiral cloistered arcade.

Recently completed, the remodeling of a Santa Monica home by architect Marc Appleton and Associates is true to the design and spirit of Mission modernist Irving Gill. The Nasatir House is inspired by Gill's design for the La Jolla Women's Club of 1913, especially in the concrete-column entrance pergola.

The Santa Fe residence of designer James Jareb reflects adventurous
design possibilities by combining contemporary New Mexican and
Moroccan decor. Strong Moorish colors are balanced by Mission-oak
furniture and ethnic folk art.

Simple wrought iron, Craftsman ceramics, and a neo-Spanish coffee table lend a Mission mood to a cozy armchair setting in the Sagal home in Los Angeles.

Predominantly a warm-weather architecture, the Mission style includes the opportunity for architects to design wonderful transitional spaces from inside rooms to outside. These transition spaces have included loggias, verandas, courtyards, patios, and balconies, all favorite devices of the Mission style. One of the West Coast's great firms, Moore Ruble Yudell of Santa Monica, employs great ingenuity in utilizing the Mission and Spanish Colonial heritage of southern California to animate the building interface between interior and exterior.

Architect Barton Phelps of Los Angeles is also attracted to the essence of the Mission style—the colors, forms, and textures—but combines them in surprising ways. Phelps's Los Angeles house may be considered a mannered expression of the Mission style, as it features abstracted and exaggerated elements such as a trapezoidal courtyard; a cutout, curvilinear parapet; and multilayered, multilevel floor plan. The complex interior spaces have a baroque richness sheathed in a sleek, modernist Mission skin of stucco. Phelps's work articulates Robert Venturi's slogan "complexity and contradiction" as it applies to Mission architecture.

In San Diego, Rob Wellington Quigley has molded Mission forms to serve his clients' desires, managing to borrow some favorite devices of Irving Gill while evoking a romantic presentation. In Quigley's work, the stark planes and arcades of Gill are softened by rich color and materials such as Mexican tiles and copper sheathing. Gill's love of geometry has also inspired Quigley.

California's innovations in neo-Mission architecture are largely unmatched by other regions. Interesting experiments in the Mission style in New Mexico have been produced by James Jareb, a connoisseur and interior designer, and L. D. Burke, a furniture designer. In Jareb's Santa Fe home, Moroccan interior style has been married to Spanish Colonial construction, perhaps a glimpse of future southwestern design trends. Burke's studio, the "Pink Church on Pacheco Street" in Santa Fe, pastes an evocative mission church facade onto an industrial-tech building of wood and corrugated metal. Both projects are inspired individual visions rather than symbols of an overall Neo-Mission architectural movement in New Mexico.

MISSION STYLE OF TOMORROW ··· The Mission style continues to surprise us with its longevity and appeal. Fully developed over a span of perhaps a thousand years, the style offers a tangible formula for graceful living that sometimes may appear as a faint desert mirage in the frenzied landscape of modern computer-age living. Cozy fireplace scenes of the bungalow; relaxed lounging in the courtyard or veranda; the comfort of a plush, oversize Morris chair; misty, tiled bathrooms that sing of the orient—all of these simple pleasures are at the heart of the Mission romance.

The great designers of the Mission Revival era fully exploited the romantic possibilities of the style, searching the vast coffers of history and geography for inspiration. Removed from the immediate overpowering influence of the Arts and Crafts movement that shaped the Mission Revival, today's Mission designers have perhaps a less-inhibited creative atmosphere to restrict their expressions.

Color, complexity, contradiction, tradition, abstraction, texture, and layering are just a few of the qualities that seem to describe the new and evolving Mission style. White walls, dark wood, and clay tiles are not the only Mission colors anymore. Present and future palettes will bloom with the full spectrum of high desert and coastal colors of Morocco, Spain, and the Southwest. The simple floor plans of Mission cottages and bungalows have exploded into living spaces that resemble complex musical compositions rather than predictable linear progressions. Maybe the most intriguing innovations in the Mission style include the redefinition of exterior and interior spaces and their relationships to each other. Patios, courtyards, and verandas will continue to grow more elaborate and exciting in the future.

The Mission style is not a passing or insignificant fancy. It embodies timeless qualities of architecture and home life that are relevant in any generation. Its rediscovery and regeneration in the 1990s has a positive reflection on the sensibilities and values of present architects, designers, and homemakers.

A new Oakland residence by Ace Architects has fun with the Craftsman-era architecture of Bernard Maybeck, who loved classical structural systems such as French Gothic. Here, a Gothic arch becomes an entire roof shell, patterned after Maybeck's design of Hearst Hall, a Berkeley landmark designed in 1899 and destroyed by fire in 1922.

ACCESSORIES ••• As the Mission style has evolved over the centuries, having acquired influences from North Africa, Spain, Mexico, and the American Southwest, it naturally has a magnificent legacy of accessories and design accents to draw upon. Some of the most ancient and traditional home furnishings of

ROMANCE OF THE MISSION STYLE

Mission-style cultures still resound powerfully in contemporary arrangements. ••• For floor and wall hangings, the incomparable tapestries of Morocco and the American Southwest add bright colors to the otherwise neutral (sometimes dark) color palette of many Mission designs. Moroccan rugs by Berber tribes, or kilims, or any Middle Eastern oriental variety such as Turkish or Persian are perfectly suited to the Mission interior, giving an Old

An antique wooden Spanish *santo*, or saint, makes a splendid table accent in the Brian Gibson House in Los Angeles.

A Prairie-style lamp on a classic trestle table with a spindle chair creates an attractive spot for study and reflection. All furnishings are by Warren Hile Studio of Sierra Madre, California.

World character. For a southwestern theme, Navajo rugs are essential.

Wrought-iron accessories are also classic Mission icons. Graceful curves of black metal translate into popular candlestick holders, table accents, light fixtures, chandeliers, and furniture hardware. Nothing quite captures the Mission aura as well as dramatic, lit candles in wrought iron.

During the Mission Revival era, hammered copper and brass became a popular medium as a counterpoint to the heavy wooden (Stickley) furniture, especially as material for lamps and other interesting home products. Best known is the work of Dirk van Erp, who invented his famous mushroom-shaped lamp of copper and mica about 1910 in San Francisco. Van Erp's style of metalworking is continued by several talented metalworkers today.

Architectural wrought iron, hammered brass and copper, and carefully selected examples of New Mexican Colonial tinwork can be common and attractive additions to most any Mission room.

The classic bungalow architecture of the Bible residence in Los Angeles
makes a perfect setting for an outstanding collection of Mission Revival-
era furnishings. In particular, the room gains distinction from a wonderful
assortment of octagonal tables, lamps, and Grueby pottery on the mantel.

Ceramics are another essential ingredient in the romantic Mission ensemble. For a historical theme, Pueblo pottery is the standard, but inspired choices can be made from the vast resources of Mexican pottery, or in California homes, from oriental examples such as Ming vases for a Monterey effect. Mission Revival style can be represented by the simple elegance of "natural" glazed pottery such as Grueby pottery or other Craftsman-style examples from the early 1900s. Contemporary designers are fond of dramatic large-scale pieces in bold Fiesta-ware colors for flamboyant flower arrangements.

The Mission-style design palette also includes other interesting materials, textures, and techniques. Heavy royal velvets for draperies, sofa cushions, and upholstery are back in vogue, lending a medieval notion of luxury. Leather is another

Warren Hile Studio's traditional slatted lamp table with tile top makes a natural partner for a hammered copper and mica lamp in the style of Dirk van Erp.

companion to Mission style, offering its unique personality to a variety of applications. Tile in all of its forms, patterns, and colors is a basic consideration. Stenciling and texturing of walls, experimenting with different color effects and techniques of pigmentation, is an evolving modern craft, although one need only study the classic missions themselves to discover a world of expression and possibilities.

Because of the many influences represented in the Mission style, the range of accessories is vast. Contemporary settings can focus upon one of these influences, such as Moroccan, Southwestern, Native American, or Spanish, or the influences can be blended for an attractive eclectic look. Whatever the direction, Mission has been and is a timeless style certain to be a design staple for generations to come.

An antique Mission sideboard acquires a New Mexican spirit when displaying fine Pueblo pottery. It's flanked with Spanish Colonial chairs by craftsman Anthony Martinez of Española, New Mexico.

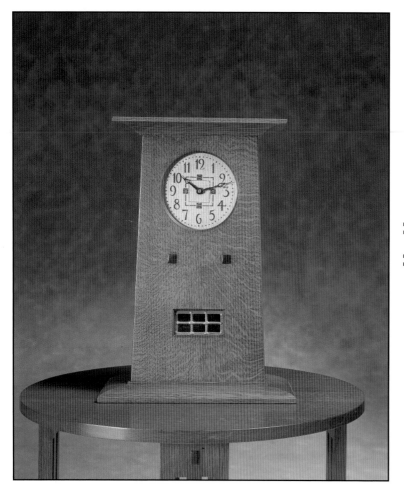

Precision clocks are a virtual symbol of the reflective nature of the
Mission style. This mantel clock
by the Stickley Company was
designed in 1912 by Peter Hansen
and remains a popular favorite.

A ceiling in the Alcazar, or royal
palace, in Sevilla displays magnificent gilded parquet woodwork.
The coat of arms of the Spanish
provinces of Castile and Aragon
are symbols of the Spanish triumph
over the Moors in 1492.

Spanish tile work found at Alcazar in Sevilla, Spain.

Thomasville Furniture offers an interesting Prairie-style hall clock with drawers as part of its American Revival collection.

A sofa by the Naturalist studio of Utah is a western variation of the Craftsman settle. The frame is constructed of alder or pine with Prairie styling and Pueblo arm accents.

The Naturalist's "Architectural Elements" sofa table is a minimal Mission table with decorative steel-inlay design and braces.

Simple slats give a Prairie edge to a modest Mission end table by the Naturalist.

A wrought-iron lamp fixture in Santa Fe artfully balances Spanish, Pueblo, and Art Deco influences.

Master craftsman and architect Lars Stanley of Austin, Texas, is one of the leading Craftsman-style blacksmiths in the United States. This English gate design contains many sublime rhythms and proportions.

Any Mission patio would be graced by John Kelly's patio furniture. The octagonal dining table has strong Craftsman-design precedents.

Craftsman Eric Freyer of Albuquerque combines New Mexican and Craftsman profiles in this contemporary Southwestern Mission table.

A set of occasional tables by Eric Freyer of Albuquerque employs clever Pueblo Deco cutout shapes for dramatic effect.

Durango chairs by Ernest Thompson Furniture of Albuquerque blend refined Craftsman styling and decorative chip-carved accents.

Sundance catalog's distinctive Mission lamp is crafted of solid copper, and the translucent mica lamp shade yields warm, honey-colored light.

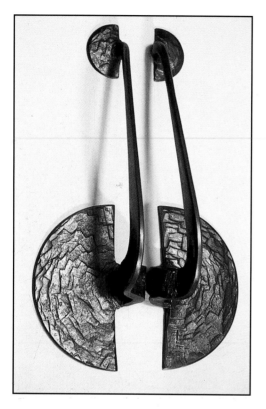

Master craftsman Lars Stanley of Austin has produced a pair of door pulls whose design seems to be an expression of natural morphology.

Elaborate wrought-iron window and door grates such as this Santa Fe example are a primal Spanish Colonial architectural expression and thus part of the Mission-design vocabulary.

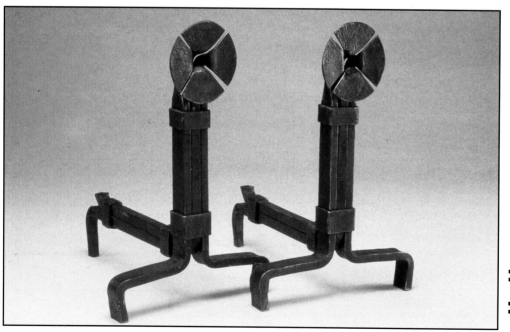

A pair of "Lotus" andirons by Austin's Lars Stanley would enhance any bungalow fireplace or Mission hearth.

Marc Coan's cherry wood and vinyl composition tile table, is a contemporary design with art deco and mission influences.

An oak and mica lamp sold by Sundance catalog is created from Gustav Stickley's original patterns.

A stained-glass lamp in the style of Frank Lloyd Wright was recently marketed by Sundance catalog.

MISSION-STYLE RESOURCES

ACCESSORIES ◆ ◆

Michael Adams
Aurora Studios
109 Main Street
Putnam, CT 06260
360-928-6662
Arts and Crafts/Lighting

V. Michael Ashford
6543 Alpine Drive SW
Olympia, WA 98502
206-352-0694
Furniture/Lighting Design

Historic Lighting
114 East Lemon Avenue
Monrovia, CA 91016
626-303-4099
Mission-style Lamps, Furniture, and Accessories

Mica Lamps
520 State Street
Glendale, CA 91203
517-241-7227
Mission-style Lamps

Sundance Catalog
Customer Service Center
P.O. Box 30307
Salt Lake City, UT 84130
800-422-2770
Mission-style Furnishings and Accessories

ANTIQUES ◆ ◆

Tim Gleason Gallery
194 Elizabeth Street #2
New York, NY 10012
212-966-5777
Fine Mission-style Antiques

Jack Moore Craftsman
Furniture
50 East Colorado Boulevard
Pasadena, CA 91105
Fine Craftsman- and Mission-style Antiques

ARCHITECTS ◆ ◆

Ace Architects
330 Second Street #1
Oakland, CA 94607
510-452-0775
Exceptional Architecture with Historical References

Marc Appleton & Associates
221 1-B Hampton Drive
Venice, CA 90291
310-399-2416
Fine Contemporary Southern California Architecture

Moore Ruble Yudell
933 Pico Boulevard
Santa Monica, CA 90405
310-450-1400
California Modernist Architecture

Barton Phelps
5514 Wilshire Boulevard
Los Angeles, CA 90036
323-934-8615
*California Architecture with
Eclectic Historical References*

Rob Wellington Quigley
434 West Cedar Street
San Diego, CA 92101
619-232-0888
*California- and Neo-Mission-
style Architecture*

CRAFTSMEN ◆ ◆

Arroyo Design
224 North 4th Avenue
Tucson, AZ 85705
520-884-1012
*Mission/Craftsman/
Biedermeier Furniture*

Berkeley Mills Studio
2830 7th Street
Berkeley, CA 94710
510-549-2854 (Berkeley)
*Oriental and Western
Craftsman Furniture*

Blue Canyon Woodworks
1310 Siler Road #1
Santa Fe, NM 87505-3104
505-471-0136
*Authentic Reproductions
of Spanish Colonial Classics*

David Burling
1 704-B Llano Street,
Suite 187
Santa Fe, NM 87505
505-466-9306
Southwest Craftsman Furniture

Marc Coan Designs
2509 Arenal SW
Albuquerque, NM 87105
505-877-5707
*Mixed-media Furniture and
Boxes*

The Craftsman's Guild
139 Alvarado Road
Berkeley, CA 94705
510-841-3111
Period/Revival/Arts and Crafts

The Craftsman Shop
528 South Fair Oaks
Pasadena, CA 91105

Due West Furniture
61 Birch Drive
Rindge, NH 03461
603-899-5259
*Contemporary
Western/Mission Furniture*

Eric Freyer Woodworks
P.O. Box 485
Sandia Park, NM 87047
505-281-4654
*Southwest Mission/Craftsman
Furniture*

Warren Hile Studio
1823 Enterprise Way
Monrovia, CA 91916
626-359-7210
*Southwest Mission/Craftsman
Furniture*

Michael Hoffer
Rt. 1, Box 381 A
Espanola, NM 87532
505-982-1763
*Redefined Southwest Mission
Furniture*

John Kelly Furniture
77 Franklin Street
New York, NY 10013
212-625-3355
*Contemporary Indoor and
Outdoor Furniture*

Livingston Furniture Design
2716 West 108th Avenue
Hutchinson, KS 67502
620-662-2781
*Spanish Colonial/Western
Fine-Art Furniture*

Mack & Rodel Cabinetmakers
44 Leighton Road
Pownal, ME 04069
207-688-4483
Craftsman Furniture

Mesilla Woodworks
1802 Avenida de Mesilla
Las Cruces, NM 88005
505-523-1362
*Southwest Mission/Craftsman
Furniture*

Jeremy Morelli Studio
540 South Guadulupe
Santa Fe, NM 87501
505-984-1587
*Nicolai Fechin Reproductions/
Native American and
Western Styles*

Thomas Moser Cabinet
Makers
72 Wright's Landing
P.O. Box 1237
Auburn, ME 14211
207-784-3332
Mission/Craftsman Furniture

The Naturalist
P.O. Box 1431
Provo, UT 84603
800-344-7244
*Contemporary
Craftsman/Mission/Western
Furniture*

Richardson Brothers
Company
P.O. Box 907
Sheboygan Falls, WI 53085
800-554-8683
*Contemporary Mission
Furniture*

Roycroft Shops
31 South Grove Street
East Aurora, NY 14052
716-652-3333
*Classic Mission/Craftsman
Furniture*

Sawbridge Studios
153 West Ohio Street
Chicago, IL 60610
312-828-0055
312-828-0066 fax
Prairie Line

Lars Stanley
P.O. Box 3095
Austin, TX 78764
512-445-0444
Craftsman-style Metalwork

L. & J. G. Stickley, Inc.
Stickley Drive
P.O. Box 480
Manlius, NY 13104
Authentic Mission/
Craftsman Furniture

Southwest Spanish Craftsman
328 South Guadalupe
Santa Fe, NM 87501
505-982-1767
Spanish Colonial/Spanish
Provincial /South west
Contemporary Furniture

Taos Furniture
1807 Second Street
P.O. Box 5555, Dept. GF
Santa Fe, NM 87502
New Mexican Colonial
Furniture with Mission
Overtones

James M. Taylor
39 Frost Hill Road
York, ME 03909
207-698-1894
Arts and Crafts Furniture

Taylor Woodcraft
Box 245, South River Road
Molta, OH 43758
740-962-3741

Mission Line
Ernest Thompson Furniture
4531 Osuna NE
Albuquerque, NM 87109
Contemporary Southwestern
and Western Furniture

Waldo Mesa Woodworks
P.O. Box 164
Cerrillos, NM 87010
505-471-1036
Contemporary New Mexican
Furniture with Mission
Overtones

Watson Heirlooms
310 West Main Street
P.O. Box 4340
Buena Vista, CO 81211
719-395-2001
Eclectic Fine Carved Furniture

Gunther Worrlein
Worrlein Studio
I I La junta Road
Lamy, NM 87540
Spanish Colonial/Southwest
Furniture

INTERIOR DESIGN ◆ ◆

Michael Anderson
Clacton and Frinton's
Anglo-American
107 South Robertson Boulevard
Los Angeles, CA 90048
310-275-1967
Fine Contemporary
Mission-style Interior Design

Roy McMakin
219 36th Avenue E
Seattle, WA 98112
206-323-6992
Domestic Furniture/Inspired
Furniture Design and interior

Design

HOTELS ◆ ◆

Beverly Hills Hotel
on Sunset Boulevard
Beverly Hills, CA 90210
310-276-2251
Luxury Mission
Revival-style Hotel

Mission Inn
3649 Mission Inn Avenue
Riverside, CA 92501
909-784-0300
A National Historic
Landmark Hotel

MANUFACTURERS ◆ ◆

Ethan Allen, Inc.
Ethan Allen Drive
Danbury, CT 06811
1-888-324-3571
American Impressions
Collections

Bassett Furniture
P.O. Box 626
Bassett, VA 24055
540-629-6000
Grove Park Mission
Collection

Thomasville Furniture Co.
P.O. Box 339
Thomasville, NC 27361
1-800-225-0265
Mission Art

PHOTOGRAPHIC CREDITS